Economic History
and the Modern Economist

Economic History
and the Modern Economist

EDITED BY
WILLIAM N. PARKER

Basil Blackwell

© William N. Parker 1986

First published 1986

Basil Blackwell Ltd
108 Cowley Road, Oxford OX4 1JF, UK

Basil Blackwell Inc.
432 Park Avenue South, Suite 1505,
New York, NY 10016, USA

British Library Cataloguing in Publication Data

Economic history and the modern economist.
1. Economic history
I. Parker, William N.
330.9   HC21

ISBN 0–631–14799–3

Library of Congress Cataloging in Publication Data

Main entry under title:
Economic history and the modern economist.

Includes index.
1. Economic history—Addresses, essays, lectures.
2. Economics—Addresses, essays, lectures. I. Parker, William Nelson.
HC26.E26   1986   330'.09   85–28584
ISBN 0–631–14799–3

Typeset by Cambrian Typesetters, Frimley, Surrey
Printed in Great Britain by Billing and Sons Ltd,
Worcester

Contents

The Contributors

The authors are professors of economics at their respective institutions:

KENNETH J. ARROW	Stanford University
PAUL A. DAVID	Stanford University
CHARLES P. KINDLEBERGER	Massachusetts Institute of Technology
DONALD N. McCLOSKEY	University of Iowa
WILLIAM N. PARKER	Yale University
W. W. ROSTOW	University of Texas at Austin
ROBERT E. SOLOW	Massachusetts Institute of Technology
PETER TEMIN	Massachusetts Institute of Technology
GAVIN WRIGHT	Stanford University

Preface

This book, slender but – we think – significant, has been formed around a discussion among economists and economic historians which took place in December 1984, at the meetings of the American Economic Association at Dallas, Texas.[1] On the program, the session was entitled, *Economic History: A Necessary though not Sufficient Condition for an Economist*.

The discussion was planned by the Association's then-President, Charles P. Kindleberger, and by me, not as an adversarial proceeding but as a frankly partisan statement. Four very well-known economists were invited to speak – two of them economic theorists and two practising economic historians. Two slightly younger – but also very well-known – economic historians were asked to prepare comments.

All the participants shared a concern felt by many economists today over the ignorance of history prevalent among social scientists, and over the indifference to that ignorance prevalent among graduate students and evident in many of the graduate programs today. The good attendance at the session, and the unusually careful attention given to the papers by the audience indicated that these concerns are more widely shared in the profession than we had supposed.

In this publication, the comments given at Dallas have been supplemented by a contributed comment from a veteran economic historian, W. W. Rostow, and a postscript from Professor Kindleberger, himself a convert to the field. As may be thought appropriate to such a topic, an historical background is offered at the beginning in the form of a short essay by the editor. It describes how economics grew up in British and American universities and how it came to neglect history, politics, and even the problems of economic policy in a pursuit of theory and measurement.

It is not our intention to present a single opinion here, or even a single view about the content of economic history or its value in the training of the 'compleat' economist. Complete unanimity is contradictory to the very goal of an educational enterprise. But the general gist and the seriousness of the issues will, we trust, become evident as a reader proceeeds in the volume. We send our efforts out into the world at large, to economists, educators, their students and their public, not merely to stimulate academic discussion but in the hope that, like all such discussions, it may lead to wise, timely and well-considered reform.

WILLIAM N. PARKER
Yale University

Note

1 A shorter, unrevised version of the papers by Arrow, Solow, David and Temin appears in the *American Economic Review, Papers and Proceedings*, vol. 75, no. 2 (May, 1985), pp. 320–37.

Acknowledgements

The authors wish to express their appreciation of the encouragement and the editorial advice and assistance of the Blackwell's editor, Elizabeth Johnson. Thanks are due also to the editor of the 1985 Papers and Proceedings volume of the *American Economic Review* from which a goodly portion of the volume has been reprinted.

1

An Historical Introduction

WILLIAM N. PARKER

In English-speaking universities today, the academic study of economic life derives from the crossing of two traditions, both honored more in the breach than in the observance. One is reminded of the polarization phenomenon in physics in which one piece of glass excluding a portion of the light spectrum is superimposed on another excluding the rest, making thus at the intersection of the two – *total darkness*!

Through British intellectual history, present-day economics traces a descent from a branch of nineteenth-century moral philosophy known to the Victorians and Edwardians as 'political economy.' Political economy – the name is still used in some British Commonwealth universities – had its famous founders: Petty, Hume, Smith, Bentham, Malthus and Ricardo; its great expositor: John Stuart Mill; and its latter day church fathers: Marshall, Pigou and Keynes. In the United States between 1880 and 1940 the tradition was, not surprisingly, reproduced at Harvard, particularly under the influence of a Middle Westerner, F. W. Taussig. Taussig's career at many points resembled that of Alfred Marshall, although his thought showed little of Marshall's subtlety, originality, or depth.

Political economy combined a rigorous intellectuality with immense moral authority, such as stemmed from so many of the creations of the eminent Victorians. The individualistic utilitarian ethic of Bentham, developed further by Mill, furnished the necessary psychological assumption (popularized as the 'economic man' or the 'rational actor'). To this

1

assumption were added certain others about the behavior of costs in the natural world. On these assumptions was constructed the rigorous classical model of Ricardo. That method and those asumptions were then extended by Jevons to create a matching theory of demand, and by Marshall in his efforts to understand the rationality of the structure of industry. The whole was given fresh life by Keynes, who despite the different assumptions that allowed him to arrive at the concept of an underemployment equilibrium, was thoroughly within the traditions of political economy, both in his concerns and in his methodology. Political economy's moral authority derived in part from the good fit which its successive models gave to the economic condition of Britain, as seen, at least from a middle-class point of view, between 1800 and 1950. Policies – free trade, the gold standard, the unbalanced budget – at one period or another seemed to be irrefutably deducible from its laws. But no less important for the subject's prestige was the nonconformist streak of genuine high-mindedness exhibited by its practitioners. The political economists were concerned with showing how businessmen maximized profits only because that activity in a competitive economy would maximize the social good. Also, they were not concerned simply or self-indulgently with the construction of complete and elegant systems of logic. Every one of these great figures from the pre-Smithian mercantilists through Keynes was concerned centrally with the problem of social welfare, as exhibited in major policy concerns of the day.

Economics today is not called political economy, except as a charming anachronism. Instead, in the United States and increasingly in Britain and the British Commonwealth, it is taken to be the most scientific of the 'social sciences.' This term looks at the subject matter through a lens quite different from that offered by political economy: a lens first manufactured not in Britain, but nineteenth-century Germany. The word 'science' was adopted in American academic jargon as the translation of the German word *Wissenschaft*, which is better translated as *knowledge*, since it is used in German without the special connotation of a 'natural science' methodology. Despite all their differences, Hegel, Marx, and later Weber, from whose work the German academy derived and maintained much of its energies, power, and authority, worked and thought, first of all, on the principle that society must be studied as a whole – not in parts under *ceteris paribus* assumptions. Along with this, they insisted that historical and social knowledge possessed a special quality not shared by natural science, in that it was acquired by human actors as they reflected on the products of human action, or on the interaction of human society with nature. Whether this reflexive quality of studies of society and psychology made for clarity or confusion – or simply for the sheer impossibility of certain knowledge at all – is itself a difficult philosophical conundrum. The extreme statement of the idea that humans have a privileged access to the understanding of human history and society by virtue of their own humanity was made by the proponents of *Verstehen* (understanding) as a path to knowledge, as in Dilthey's famous statement: *'Die Natur erklären wir; das Seelenleben verstehen wir.'*[1] The German academy also derived authority among the founders of the 'scientific' school of historical studies in America through a methodological principle of the opposite sort: the principle of sticking to the 'facts,' of telling history 'as it really was' (*wie es eigentlich gewesen*) – a principle that fitted well with the empirical and pragmatic bent of American philosophy.

The superimposition of these two intellectual traditions, British political economy and German historical economics, created American academic economics. The labor was long and the birth pangs were not easy. The British tradition was followed at Harvard and to a degree at Yale and Chicago, being unsettled at the two latter schools by the powerful, but temporary and more Germanic, influences of W. G. Sumner at Yale and, less markedly, of Thorstein Veblen in his years at Chicago. British 'classical' political economy was taught from the texts of Mill, Marshall and later Taussig; elements of marginalism and neo-classicism, largely through Marshall and a few of his American contemporaries, were allowed to penetrate. But the emphasis was on a study which, by laying bare 'economic principles,' served as a guide to 'policy' – to liberal policy to clear the ground for the free operation of markets, to active social policy in cases of market failure. At the new state universities from 1890 on, it was the influence of the German schools of social science and history which was paramount, and the American worship of the Ph.D. degree and title became enshrined. Veblen in particular gave the German bent of thinking, both its holism and its empiricism, unforgettably vivid and penetrating expression. To his influence was added the powerful influence of the native American pragmatists, Peirce, Dewey and their epigoni.

The 'native' school of American economics developing between 1910 and 1945 was called 'institutionalism.' Its prophet was Veblen and its law-giver was John R. Commons, the Wisconsin institutionalist who was himself an institution. From its economists and law professors at Wisconsin, California, Texas, Columbia and Cornell derived much of the regulatory legislation of that period, down through and including the New Deal agencies – the AAA, the SEC and the Social Security Administration. In the universities and research institutes, it developed in two main branches. One group of writers attacked American capitalism and devoted books and careers in the university and in public life to the institutional reform of American society. The other – more academic – pursued what Veblen thought of as the 'evolutionary' approach: the collection of facts about modern society which would show empirically, and without British (or French) hypothetico-deductive methods, the course of modern economies moving through history, their oscillations and their trends. This effort occupied the energies of the empirical Institutionalists, the conservative wing under Wesley Mitchell and following him, Simon Kuznets, Raymond Goldsmith and the long line of

4

scholars, both distinguished and conscientious, at the National Bureau of Economic Research.

Now in the late 1930s, the sudden impact of Keynes's *General Theory* caused political economy itself to divide into its 'micro' and 'macro' components. Keynesian political economists took over the income and product measurements of the National Bureau, and resolving all economic problems into that of providing full employment, they produced a universal remedy through manipulation of the federal budget. The greater part of the institutionalists' concern with economic structures was shoved aside and with the conquest of the business cycle, economic history presumably came to an end. Non-Keynesian political economists, following the lead of J. R. Hicks, and encouraged by the successful applications of planning models in wartime programs, continued the march toward a theory of general equilibrium, arriving at their goal by extending the marginal principle to everything under the sun. Maximization through equalization at the margin 'subject to constraints' became the universal law of economic life and the mathematical expression of the system by the nineteenth-century continental economist, Walras, was reproduced and elegantly elaborated.[2] American institutionalism gave an agonised last cry through the lips and in the books of J. K. Galbraith. Economists winced at the sarcasms – some of them worthy of Veblen himself, and returned to what they considered more useful and more constructive labors.

The issue of these intellectual currents appeared in the graduate training of young economists in universities in both the American- and the British-derived systems. Before 1950 graduate schools, many of them still requiring a reading knowledge of French and German for the Ph.D., had as a standard requirement oral or written examinations in three 'basic fields' and one or two 'applied fields.' The basic fields were called economic theory (incorporating the Ricardian tradition as amplified by Marshall), economic history (blending institutionalism with a brand of Germano–British historical empiricism) and statistics (less emphasized in Britain but thought essential in America for 'handling' quantitative data). The applied fields, in which choice was allowed, included the well-known menu: money and banking (which by this time had already begun to mean Keynesian theory), public finance (ditto), industrial organization (not yet a mere application of 'micro' but still a blend of Marshall and Veblen with policy emphasis on anti-trust), international trade (which tried mysteriously to blend the 'pure' theory – two countries, two commodities, no factor movements, etc. – with the facts of real world history and tariff policy) and a number of others.

After 1950, the emphasis in this menu shifted to what continued to be called economic theory. Economists in the prosperity of the 1950s and 1960s gained great prestige, and the subject came to be regarded as the paradigm of the social sciences, a science on the plan of ninteenth-century physics, with simple, rigorous mechanical models, tested from an abundance of numerical data by use of advanced, mathematically expressed formulae, based largely on the theory of probability as elaborated in the developing art of mathematical statistics. If economics was the queen of the social sciences, the the queen of economics was 'theory' and its handmaiden was econometrics.

The use of the singular number in the phrase economic theory indeed is significant, as if there were only one theory – one God in perhaps two persons: micro and macro; if not one single theorem, then at least one mode of thought, and that best expressed by the concepts and symbols of mathematics, abstract and simple though they must be. The fact that micro and macro theory do not fit very well together, that the conditions postulated in general equilibrium theory are not even approached in the world we know, that governments, politics and social movements intervene and interfere dazzlingly in the world's economies – all such problems did not form the agenda for theorizing, but instead were subordinated through simplifying assumptions to the construction of theory of

6

unerring rigor and logical accuracy, based largely on free markets and individual choice. Disturbing considerations were said to lie 'outside economics' since they lay in areas where the economist's received theory, and developing econometric techniques yielded no special advantage. In the United States and increasingly in British and British Commonwealth universities, economics departments began to resemble schools of engineering, and of a very narrow kind; schools of business administration indeed looked to departments of economics for topics and personnel.

And so it came to be that the post-war scientistic *Zeitgeist* selected out in 'micro' or in 'macro' form just those elements from political economy and institutionalism which could combine into a 'hard' science – the hypothetico-deductive rationalism of eighteenth- and nineteenth-century political economy, and the statistical empiricism which was incorporated with a social idealism in German and American institutionalist thought. What was abandoned was the humane interest of the British political economy in economic policy asnd social welfare, and the idealistic (though in the long-run sense truly realistic) German historical economist's concern for the whole society – the setting of the study of economic activities within a history and sociology of capitalism.

As a consequence, in graduate programs over the past 25 years, theory has come to be elevated to a central place while being itself more and more narrowly and 'rigorously' defined. Econometrics is no doubt a great improvement over plain vanilla statistics; still for practical problems both theory and econometrics remain but the humblest, if the most arcane, of instruments. The institutional content, the social concepts, the moral zeal implicit in the training which economists used to be given through courses in economic history, economic institutions, and applied fields have been pushed aside while these fields have themselves been partially transformed or distorted into playgrounds for the imagination of the theorist. Their informational content has been neglected as unimportant, if

7

not wholly abandoned. Yet it is just this content and these concerns – and not its perfectly generalizable methodology for handling data and problems – that distinguish economics as a specialized branch among the studies of society.

As an incident in this warfare against the intellect, the field called the 'history of economic thought,' which economists used to delight in calling the 'history of thought,' a field whose subject matter and personalities once formed a part of the basic culture of every economist, is now almost completely defunct – partly because, as a subject in intellectual history, it is simply too difficult, too subtle, too tangled for busy economists to master, and partly because its practitioners have exhibited the awkward habit of pointing out that no theoretical system has ever avoided the erosion of time. Like all historical subjects, its principle lesson is summed up in the Persian wise man's one phrase of universal applicability: 'And this too shall pass away.' Like all absolute rulers, economists have answered the philosopher by chopping off his head.

To a degree, the field called 'economic history' – though clearly an endangered species in modern economics programs – has survived these decades with much of its original quality intact. The fascination of two decades of economic historians with quantification and the use of theory has strengthened the field without in the end strangling it. Perhaps the reason is that economic history seems to mean many things to many people. Yet the conjunction of all its definitions, which are mutually supportive rather than contradictory, is an amorphous body of scholars and scholarship, exposure to which offers to the young economist a rich and novel experience. It says in Hamlet's words to Horatio: 'There are more things in heaven and earth . . . than are dreamt of in your philosophy.' For giving this lesson, if for no other reason, economic history is an important ingredient in an economist's education.

But there are other reasons. Economic history forms in fact one leg of the chair on which an educated economist must sit to do useful work. Without some knowledge of the field, its methods and its problems, an economist misses one dimension in his training – a dimension with qualities of both breadth and depth. Such an economist becomes a shallower, narrower analyst with feeble capabilities for adapting the theory and statistics he has mastered to new and strange social environments. All problems strike such a one as new – isolated in space and time, whereas in fact, most problems have analogies, counterparts, precedents. A simple awareness of this fact can add immeasurably to the depth of an economist's perceptions. Without history's materials and the economic intuition deriving from familiarity with them, theory feeds upon itself, models become artificial and involuted, hypotheses become unreal. If stripped of the materials and craftsmanlike methods of economic history, economics will become an ornamental, rather than a useful, art.

Then the role of economist as it has been known – of a thoughtful analyst of economic problems and phenomena, of a scholar of penetration, range and depth – will fall empty. It will be filled, because a modern civilization needs economists, as it needs political scientists and historians to help it understand itself, and to give wise counsel for pressing problems. If truly applied economics and economic history disappear from economics departments, they will live to rise again elsewhere – in schools of public policy, business, law and international relations. They will reappear because they are needed to complement those studies of the other aspects of society's life. Without attention to history, to policy, to the range of social studies, economists will be left on the side, paddling a canoe around cool, mathematical backwaters. Someday they may awake to find that the stream of social life and social study – with its excitement, its turbulence, its freshness, its power – has passed them by.

Notes

1 We *explain* Natural phenomena, but of the life of the Spirit we have an inner *understanding*.

9

2   On this paragraph, Paul David comments: '. . . general equilibrium theory came to be more deeply understood in its own terms, even though it could not readily be reconciled with the demand-side phenomena upon which macroeconomists – who had lost their long-term interest in the supply side of growth – were concerned. Hence the supply side of growth reappeared in the guise of the simplest of general equilibrium models, the one-sector Swan–Solow growth models. It thus lost its former connections with real world institutions, because general equilibrium theory had moved away from such concerns.'

Economics and Economic History: the Record of a Discussion

2

History: the View from Economics

KENNETH J. ARROW

Henry David Thoreau said about the newly invented telegraph: 'They tell us that Maine can now communicate with Texas. But does Maine have anything to say to Texas?' This panel – its location here in Dallas and the affiliations of its members show that indeed California and Massachusetts, at least, have much to say in Texas and perhaps to Texas as well. But, as Dante explained so long ago, we must interpret texts not merely literally but also allegorically and even spiritually. Let Maine and Texas be interpreted, then, to be economic analysis and economic history – though not necessarily respectively. Our task here, as I understand it, is to consider the importance to both of maintaining the telegraph wire between them.

I use the term, 'analysis,' rather than, 'theory,' because I want to contrast the aims of history and those of social science. Permit me to use the changes in my own thinking as illustration. I always found history very interesting and read heavily in it. As a graduate student, I qualified in economic history, which was compulsory, and never felt it to be an intrusion, as later generations of students have sometimes felt. Then, later, as a faculty member at Stanford, I had to consider the role of economic history in the curriculum, and the problem of filling vacancies there. I took it for granted that history was a necessity but recognized the difficulty of finding scholars who were both economists and historians. This was in the early 1950s, before a new generation solved that supply problem. I assumed, too, that the role of history in the education of economists was to furnish evidence on a par with contemporary empirical evidence. To study history was, I supposed, a part of the job of testing theories. This view was reinforced by what was then the most significant use of history in economics: Simon Kuznets's development of long time series on national income and its components, with their strong implications for understanding the movements of the consumption function and the whole process of long-run economic development.

A lecture by the University of Chicago historian, Leonard Krieger, around 1957 changed my view of the nature of history. This was a time of much discussion regarding the role of social science in history in general and Krieger was regarded as an historian sympathetic to social science. Still, in his lecture he made clear that history could not be regarded simply as a branch of social science. Its aims were different. It sought to study the individual case, he said, while social science aimed at general principles. A social science, economics or another, might indeed be useful, even vital, in interpreting a past event. Certainly, psychological theories of different kinds have been used – though possibly not always with the best results – in interpreting the behavior of political leaders. But the aim of historical study was not simply to serve as a source of data from which to infer and to test social science generalizations. For the historian, the social sciences were tools to help him illuminate the particular event. This view does not, of course, preclude the use of the data produced by historical investigations for the purposes of socio-scientific analysis. The two modes of inquiry are complements, not substitutes. But they are not identical.

Let me draw an analogy from the natural world as it is studied in the science of geology. The underlying laws of geology are simply the standard laws of physics and chemistry. There is, from the viewpoint of scientific generalizations, nothing peculiar to geology.[1] That water wears down rocks, that heat sources in the interior of the Earth can produce great changes in the Earth's surface, that the energy of the Earth derives in major part but not entirely from solar radiation, that under high temperatures and pressures the materials of the Earth form new chemical combinations – these relations and others have determined the course of the Earth's development. Further, examination of the history of the Earth could in principle yield evidence about the measurements of specific chemical and physical reactions. In practice, however, observation in the laboratory is so much more efficient that the evidence of geological observation has been of little use to the underlying sciences except to suggest research problems.

But geology is a flourishing subject, and much of its interest is in the specific historical event. What is the history of the Appalachians and the Himalayas? What have been the movements of the Indian subcontinent? Why does Hawaii have the shape it does? Geology is in good measure a study of the specific. Geology is an historical study and a fascinating one.

The example of geology illustrates a recurrent topic in economics. Is economics a subject like physics, true for all time, or are its laws historically conditioned? The study of history was on the rise throughout the nineteenth century, even while the abstract economic theory of David Ricardo was developed. Ricardo's doctrines were attacked by his contemporaries for their lack of historical content and understanding. His disciple, John Stuart Mill, made clear that the laws of distribution were indeed historically conditioned, that the classical laws of value held only in an economy in which exchange was governed by markets. In the same way the theory of plate tectonics is historically conditioned. It is a valid statement about the Earth today and over a long period in the past. It could not have held when the Earth was excessively hot, and it may or may not be true for other planets.

Physics and chemistry have clearly been very useful to geology, interpreted as history. What does standard economic theory have to contribute to economic history? It could fail on several grounds. Theory might be so overwhelmingly powerful that history would become uninteresting, merely the playing

15

out of a well-defined script. Or it could be so wrong as to constitute an obstacle to historical understanding. W. J. Cunningham, for example, writing about 1890, attacked Ricardo and Marshall for interpreting rent in the Tudor period in Ricardian terms, not recognizing the differences in historical conditions.

The first failing – the excessive power of the theory – is clearly not relevant, though some economic theorists have spoken as if it were. In form, neo-classical theory is a statement of the implications which tastes, technology and expectations have for the prices and quantities observed on markets. (Other variations of economic theory have a similar form, though different content.) There would be plenty of room for historical specificity in the conditions even if economic theory were more reliable than it is in drawing conclusions from them. There is nothing in economic theory which specifies that tastes remain unchanged, and we have now a great deal of empirical knowledge about changes in technology. Indeed, it may be complained rather that economic theory does not sufficiently constrain the interpretation of historical movements, particularly when the data are not sufficient to test its models.

It would be widely accepted, I think, that the ideas and approaches of economic theory have been useful in economic history. Economic theory has raised new questions for history. It helps the historian to ask not merely how economic institutions are supposed to work, but how in fact they *do* work in redirecting the flow of resources. Our views of the relations between railroads and economic growth in the nineteenth century, of the diffusion of specific technological innovations such as the reaper, of the economic consequences and functioning of slavery have all been seriously altered in ways that required new ways of thinking and suggested search for new kinds of evidence. Measuring the economic conditions of the masses of the population has been driven perhaps by political aims as much as by the considerations of modern welfare economics, but the appropriate measures and data have certainly been much clarified by the latter. I have already alluded to Kuznets's long time series on national income, a concept drawn from economic analysis, as a major contribution to our understanding both of the constancies and the structural changes of the past.

The example of national income analysis reminds us of a danger in the use of economic theory in economic history. Theory contains a bias towards flattening out the particularities of the past. The more one uses general categories to satisfy a need to generalize, the more one neglects 'irrelevant' differences among the specific cases, the instantiations of the general statement. This is not a logical consequence of the use of theoretical constructs. As already emphasized, each historical episode can in principle be interpreted as the application of general propositions to unique contexts; but the bias drawn from theory is likely to emphasize generality at the expense of particularity. One is reminded of earlier modes of historical interpretation, in which every catastrophe was attributed to the workings of the hand of God. Many theories for the interpretation of myths, for example, tend to consider them as illustrations of some general principle – Frazer's dying king, Muller's rising and setting sun, Freud's Oedipus complex, or the modern structuralist's universal form. What is lost in such general interpretations is the sense that myths are different; it simply is not true that when you've heard one, you've heard them all.

What about the uses of history in the development of economic analysis? There are many, but let me pick two, both alluded to earlier. One is the use of economic history as a source of empirical evidence for testing theories and estimating relations. I referred to this earlier as my 'naïve' view on the role of history. It is far from exhausting the content of history, but it is certainly one of its uses. When an examination of long time series shows, as Summers has recently told us, that interest rates do not fully adjust to compensate for inflation, the routine acceptance of the Fisher effect in the analysis of

17

contemporary conditions must surely be questioned. The regular patterns of consumption described by Engel's laws can be confirmed by historical shifts in industrial structure as well as by budget studies, making it hard, incidentally, to maintain simple models of homogeneous economic growth. Studies of past hyperinflations and their endings test theories of inflation. The historical analysis of individual business cycles was a live field after the pioneering work of Walt Rostow from 1946 to about 1960; it was neglected because of one-sided theories, first Keynesian and then monetarist, but I hope Peter Temin's work signals a revival. Such work is both history itself and a testing-ground for the many relations which define cyclical fluctuations.

A second use of history in the development of economic analysis is – as alluded to earlier – a definition of its historical conditioning. Before economic analysis had much effect on economic history, historians debated whether and which earlier periods could be described as capitalist or almost so. The great classical historian, M. I. Rostovtzeff, found the early Roman Empire to be governed by modern economic institutions, factor mobility, profit seeking, and all the rest. He has been ridiculed for this by the current leading authority, Moses Finley, who finds little evidence of rational economic behavior in the ancient world. Again, Henri Pirenne found merchants and traders in a few centuries around the year 1000 to have been thorough-going profit seekers, acutely sensitive to price differences; but the crystallization of the guild system, according to Pirenne, subsequently created a different economic world. It is not for the theorists to assess the very specialized evidence available. Still, there is some suggestion that the economic world of the past was not entirely different from that of our theories, for example, in the sharp rise in real wages after the radical shift in the land–labor ratio occasioned by the Black Death.

Closely intertwined with the historical conditioning of theory is the national or cultural conditioning. The study of one area's

18

past resembles in some respects the study of a variety of present-day conditions as they appear in other parts of the world. Very large differences appear to exist even among capitalist countries in such basic economic variables as savings rates and rates and levels of productivity growth. Even between such economically and culturally similar nations as the United States and Canada, significant differences appear in per capita incomes, productivity (even controlling for capital equipment, as in the automobile industry), and labor union membership and activity. When we go farther afield, the differences increase. Studies have shown, for example, that real wage flexibility is distinctly lower in Western Europe than in the United States. As between Japan and the United States, differences appear in industrial organization even under virtually identical technologies. Large Japanese corporations perform innovative tasks which in America seem best done by small firms. Perhaps widely alleged differences in organizational loyalty and the role of consensus in decision making within the large firm are a factor.

Cross-country comparisons of this kind are analogous to historical comparisons in exploring the range of validity of economic generalizations. But the relation is deeper. Presumably, the international differences, in so far as they are not simply explainable by differences in natural resources, are themselves the result of history. Political scientists have suggested, for example, that important differences between the United States and Canada may be traced back to the fact that the United States was created by the American Revolution while the political constitution of English-speaking Canada was in part a reaction to that event. The cultural differences between nations, with all their implications for policy and economy, are precipitates of events in the past, sometimes in the distant past. In an ideal theory, perhaps, the whole influence of the past would be summed up in observations on the present. But such a theory cannot be stated in any complex uncontrolled system, not even for the Earth, as we have seen.

19

It will always be true that practical understanding of the present will require knowledge of the past.

Note

1 Since presenting this paper, I have learned that the analogy between economics and geology had already been drawn by S. Rashid, 'Political Economy and Geology in the Early Nineteenth Century: Similarities and Contrasts,' *History of Political Economy*, vol. 13 (1981), pp. 726–44.

3

Economics: Is Something Missing?

ROBERT E. SOLOW

I have in the back of my mind a picture of the sort of discipline economics ought to be – or at least the sort of discipline I wish it were. If economics were practiced in that way there would be nothing problematical about its reciprocal relationship with economic history. It would be pretty clear what economic theory offers to economic history and what economic history offers to economic theory. I will try to describe what I mean in a minute.

For better or worse, however, economics has gone down a different path, not the one I have in mind. One consequence, not the most important one, but the one that matters for this discussion, is that economic theory learns nothing from economic history, and economic history is as much corrupted as enriched by economic theory. I will come to that too, later on.

You will notice that I am using strong language. I am prepared to admit right away that I may be dead wrong, in my judgments. But there is no point in pussyfooting. Bluntness may lead to an interesting discussion.

To get right down to it, I suspect that the attempt to construct economics as an axiomatically based hard science is doomed to fail. There are many, partially overlapping, reasons for believing this; but since that is not the topic under discussion today, I do not have to lay them out in an orderly way. I hope the following hodge-podge will convey what I mean.

A modern economy is a very complicated system. Since we cannot conduct controlled experiments on its smaller parts, or even observe them in isolation, the classical hard-science devices for discriminating between competing hypotheses are closed to us. The main alternative device is the statistical analysis of historical time series. But then another difficulty arises. The competing hypotheses are themselves complex and subtle. We know before we start that many of them are capable of fitting the data in a gross sort of way. Then, in order to make more refined distinctions, we need *long* time series observed under *stationary* conditions.

Unfortunately, however, economics is a social science. It is subject to Damon Runyon's law that nothing between human beings is more than three to one. To express the point more formally, much of what we observe cannot be treated as the realization of a stationary stochastic process without straining credulity. Morover, all narrowly economic activity is entangled in a web of social institutions, customs, beliefs and attitudes. Outcomes are indubitably affected by these background factors, some of which change slowly and gradually, others erratically. As soon as time series get long enough to offer hope of discriminating among complex hypotheses, the likelihood that they remain stationary diminishes, and the noise level gets correspondingly high. Under these circumstances, a little cleverness and persistence can get you almost any result you want. I think that that explains why so few econometricians have ever been forced by the facts to abandon a firmly held belief. Indeed some of Fortune's favorites have been known to write scores of empirical articles without once feeling obliged to report a result that contradicts their prior prejudices.

I am not prepared to abandon the exhaustive study of the implications of particular axiom systems, though I admit that I do not expect a lot from that sort of theory. What I am arguing against is the foolish belief that when it comes to studying the real world there is only one useful system of axioms and we already know what it is.

If I am anywhere near right about this, the interests of scientific economics would be better served by a more modest approach. There is enough for us to do without pretending to a degree of completeness and precision which we cannot deliver. To my way of thinking, the true functions of analytical economics are best described informally: to organize our necessarily incomplete perceptions about the economy, to see connections that the untutored eye would miss, to tell plausible – sometimes even convincing – causal stories with the help of a few central principles, and to make rough quantitative judgments about the consequences of economic policy and other exogenous events. In this scheme of things, the end-product of economic analysis is likely to be a collection of models contingent on society's circumstances – on the historical context, you might say – and not a single monolithic model for all seasons.

I hope no one here will think that this low-key view of the nature of analytical economics is a license for loose thinking. Logical rigor is just as important in this scheme of things as it is in the more self-consciously scientific one. The same goes for econometric depth and sophistication, maybe even more so. I mentioned 'rough' quantitative judgment a moment ago, but that was only to suggest that the best attainable, in macro-economics anyway, is not likely to be precise, if we are honest with ourselves and others. It would be a useful principle that economists should actually believe the empirical assertions they make. That would require more discipline than most of us now exhibit, when many empirical papers seem more like virtuoso finger exercises than anything else. The case I am trying to make concerns the scope and ambitions of economic model building, not the intellectual and technical standards of model building.

I claimed earlier that the natural relation between economics and economic history would be clear and straighforward if only economics were practiced in the fashion I have just sketched. Now I had better say what I meant. If economists set

23

themselves the task of modelling particular contingent social circumstances, with some sensitivity to context, it seems to me that they would provide exactly the interpretive help an economic historian needs. That kind of model is directly applicable in organizing a historical narrative, the more so to the extent that the economist is conscious of the fact that different social contexts may call for different background assumptions and therefore for different models.

The other direction of influence – what economic history offers to that kind of economic theory – is more interesting. If the proper choice of a model depends on the institutional context – and it should – then economic history performs the nice function of widening the range of observation available to the theorist. Economic theory can only gain from being taught something about the range of possibilities in human societies. Few things should be more interesting to a civilised economic theorist than the opportunity to observe the interplay between social institutions and economic behavior over time and place.

I am going to illustrate by referring to the work of W. H. B. Court, and not merely because his book *The Rise of the Midland Industries* was on A. P. Usher's reading list when I took his course in the late 1940s. I choose Court for no better reason than that I happened to run across an obituary article about him in the *Proceedings* of the British Academy for 1982. (Since Court died in 1971, fate did seem to be playing a hand.)

Here, for instance, is an excerpt from Court's volume on *Coal* in the UK's official history of the Second World War.

> Observers who found the conduct of the mineworkers puzzling assumed that, in the normal way, a man who finds himself faced with the possibilities of higher earnings will be prepared to put out extra effort to obtain them. An assumption about the conduct of an individual is as a rule, however, also an assumption in some sort about the society in which he lives and of which he is a member. The individual's demand for income, his views upon the getting and spending of money, are usually formed by the part of society which he is most in touch with.

For most men the social code, whatever it may be in their time and place, is something which they accept as given and take over with little demur or questioning. Before one can assume that a demand for additional income existed on the coalfields and could easily translate itself into extra work, one has to ask whether the mining community had those standards or those habits. If it did not, and if it was unable to develop them in a short time, then even a rapid rise of wage rates might bring about no appreciable change in the working habits of the industry.

In his own methodological writing, Court made the point explicitly that men 'living as they do in different societies . . . make their decisions according to different schemes of values and according to the habits and structures of the society they find themselves living in.' Therefore an economic historian should be an 'observer and re-creator of the codes, loyalties and organizations which men create and which are just as real to them as physical conditions.' Add to that a command over two-stage least squares and you have the kind of economic historian from whom theorists have most to learn, if only they are willing to try. I have naturally lit on this passage about the labor market because that is the branch of theory I happen to be engaged in right now, but no doubt the thought would apply equally well to consumer spending or rivalry among firms. I must promise myself, before I lecture again on wage bargaining, to ask my students to read the chapters on 'The Wage Bargain' and 'The Concept of the Minimum' in Court's *British Economic History, 1870–1914: Commentary and Documents*. I wonder what they will make of it.

So much for the normative. If you read the same journals as I do, you may have noticed that modern economics has an ambition and style rather different from those I have been advocating. My impression is that the best and brightest in the profession proceed as if economics is the physics of society. There is a single universally valid model of the world. It only needs to be applied. You could drop a modern economist from a time machine – a helicopter, maybe, like the one that drops the money – at any time, in any place, along with his or her personal computer; he or she could set up in business without even bothering to ask what time and which place. In a little while, the up-to-date economist will have maximized a familiar-looking present-value integral, made a few familiar log-linear approximations, and run the obligatory familiar regression. The familiar coefficients will be poorly determined, but about one in twenty of them will be significant at the 5 percent level, and the other nineteen do not have to be published. With a little judicious selection here and there, it will turn out that the data are just barely consistent with your thesis adviser's hypothesis that money is neutral (or non-neutral, take your choice) everywhere and always, modulo an information asymmetry, any old information asymmetry, don't worry, you'll think of one.

All right, so I exaggerate. You will recognize the kernel of truth in the cartoon. We are socialized to the belief that there is one true model and that it can be discovered or imposed if only you will make the proper assumptions and impute validity to econometric results that are transparently lacking in power.

Of course there are holdouts against this routine, bless their hearts.

As I inspect some current work in economic history I have the sinking feeling that a lot of it looks exactly like the kind of economic analysis I have just finished caricaturing: the same integrals, the same regressions, the same substitution of t-ratios for thought. Apart from anything else, it is no fun reading the stuff any more. Far from offering the economic theorist a widened range of perceptions, this sort of economic history gives back to the theorist the same routine gruel that the economic theorist gives to the historian. Why should I believe, when it is applied to thin eighteenth-century data, something that carries no conviction when it is done with more ample twentieth-century data?

The situation reminds me of a story I once heard told by an

anthropologist who had spent some months recording the myths and legends of a group of Apache in New Mexico. One night, just before she was scheduled to end her field work and depart, the Indians said to her: 'We have been telling you our legends all these months – why don't you tell us one of yours?' The anthropologist thought fast and then responded brilliantly by telling the Indians a version of the story of Beowulf. Years later she picked up a copy of an anthropological journal and found in the table of contents an article entitled 'On the Occurrence of a Beowulf-like legend among the such-and-such Apache.' If economic history turns into something that could be described as 'The Occurrence of an Overlapping-Generations-like Legend among the Seventeenth-century Neapolitans' then we are at the point where economics has nothing to learn from economic history but the bad habits it has taught to economic history.

Let me recapitulate. If the project of turning economics into a hard science could succeed, it would surely be worth doing. No doubt some of us should keep trying. If it did succeed, then there would be no difference between economics and economic history other than the source of data, no more than there is a difference between the study of astronomical events taking place now and those that took place in the Middle Ages. In this dispensation an economic historian is merely an economist with a high tolerance for dust and possibly – what is rarer these days – a working knowledge of a foreign language.

There are, however, some reasons for pessimism about the project. Hard sciences dealing with complex systems – but possibly less complex than the US economy – like the hydrogen atom or the optic nerve seem to succeed because they can isolate, they can experiment, and they can make repeated observations under controlled conditions. Other sciences, like astronomy, succeed because they can make long series of observations under natural but essentially stationary conditions, and because the forces being studied are not swamped by noise. Neither of these roads to success is open to economics.

27

There is, of course, a growing body of 'experimental economics.' It is used to study bargaining and other forms of market behavior, usually for small sums and by small groups of people. It is too soon to know if results obtained in this way are replicable in other 'laboratories' or applicable in real economic life. The research is certainly to be encouraged. In the immediate context I am thinking primarily about macro-economics, where replicable experimentation is more or less out of the question. How could we replicate in a laboratory a set of memories, beliefs and expectations about the behavior of the Federal Reserve System? How could we even know that experimental subjects believe that the laboratory's monetary policy is really produced by the real Fed? I grant that it is the job of an imaginative experimenter to provide satisfactory answers to or circumventions of such questions or – as Charles Plott has pointed out to me – to reduce them to more elementary questions that are susceptible of experiment. I am all for trying, but I am allowed to be skeptical.

In that case we need a different approach. The function of the economist in this approach is still to make models and test them as best one can, but the models are more likely to be partial in scope and limited in applicability. 'Testing' will have to be less mechanical and more opportunistic, encompassing a broader collection of techniques. One will have to recognize that the validity of an economic model may depend on the social context. What is here today may be gone tomorrow, or if not tomorrow then in ten or twenty years' time. In this dispensation there is a clear and productive division of labor between the economist and the economic historian. The economist is concerned with making and testing models of the economic world as it now is, or as we think it is. The economic historian can ask whether this or that story rings true when applied in earlier times or other places, and, if not, why not. So the economic historian can use the tools provided by the economist but will need, in addition, the ability to imagine how things might have been before they became as they now are.

28

These are the sensitivities Court spoke of in the passage quoted earlier. I take it, naively perhaps, that they represent the comparative advantage of the historian.

In return, economic history can offer the economist a sense of the variety and flexibility of social arrangements and thus, in particular, a shot at understanding a little better the interaction of economic behavior and other social institutions. That strikes me as a meaningful division of labor. It was once suggested – by my kind of economist – that the division of labor is limited by the extent of the market. Perhaps what I have just been doing can be thought of as suggesting that economists extend their market and accept the specialized services that, in a more capacious market, the historians as well as other scholars, can provide.

4

Understanding the Economics of QWERTY: the Necessity of History

Cicero demands of historians, first, that we tell true stories. I intend fully to perform my duty on this occasion, by giving you a homely piece of narrative economic history in which 'one damn thing follows another.' The main point of the story will become plain enough: it is sometimes not possible to uncover the logic (or illogic) of the world around us except by understanding how it got that way. A *path-dependent* sequence of economic changes is one in which important influences upon the eventual outcome can be exerted by temporally remote events, including happenings dominated by chance elements rather than systematic forces. Stochastic processes like that do not converge automatically to a fixed-point distribution of outcomes, and are called *non-ergodic*. In such circumstances 'historical accidents' can neither be ignored, nor neatly quarantined for the purposes of economic analysis; the dynamic process itself takes on an *essentially historical* character.

Standing alone, my story will be simply illustrative and does not establish how much of the world works this way. That is an open empirical issue and I would be presumptuous to claim to have settled it, or to instruct you in what to do about it. Let us just hope the tale proves mildly diverting to those waiting to hear if and why the study of economic history is a necessity in the making of good economists.

By now you know that I want to dodge the question of the place of economic history courses in the proper training of economists. But before plunging ahead, I suppose I had better confess my reason for not seriously confronting the pedagogical issues raised by the statement that history is a necessary though not sufficient condition for the making of an economist: I suffer from what is undoubtedly a socially inappropriate reaction to the absurd state of affairs which seems to call for such reaffirmations. I get a mild case of the giggles. It puts me in mind of nothing so much as the title of a book written by James Thurber and E. B. White, *circa* 1929: *Is Sex Necessary? or Why You Feel the Way You do.*[1] Now I imagine there are others who have a different, more embarrassed reaction when this topic is brought up. If you are a straight economist and public mention of the subject of instruction in economic history does leave you feeling edgy, let me suggest that you can make these proceedings more comfortable by substituting 'Sex' for 'History.' Whatever else happens, this should help you to keep your bearings – which often is difficult to do once you get deep into a methodological discussion. The other thing you can try is to remember that the economic historians among you today are not alien creatures, but 'flesh of your flesh,' so to speak. Being children of the parent discipline of Economics, they are as much the subjects for condolences as for congratulations. Upon them the gods too often have visited the sins of the fathers. I'll talk about that problem another time, however.

Actually, if now we have agreed upon the notation: economists = 'parents,' economic historians = 'children,' and history = 'sex,' what Thurber and White's book has to say is quite suitable to the present occasion. I refer to the beginning of their chapter VI, entitled 'What Should Children Tell Parents?', which runs along these lines. 'Many *children* come to me with the question, "What am I to tell my *parents* about *sex*?" My answer is always this: "Tell them the truth. When one approaches the subject in a tactful way, teaching a *parent* about *sex* should be no more embarrassing than giving instruction in personal pronouns. And it is less discouraging." '

Why not let economists find out about history in their own

good time, instead of going through the awkwardness of trying to tell them about it? Thurber and White offered a candid answer, along the following lines: 'One's *parents* are never too old to be told facts. Indeed to keep them in ignorance is quite cruel, for it allows them to nourish the doubts and horrors of their imagination. The majority of *parents* pick up their information about *sex* from smoking-car conversations, bridge-club teas, and after-dinner speakers. They receive it from their vicious adult companions who are only scarcely less ignorant than they are and who give them a dreadfully garbled version of what they should know.'

If economists are not to be left to pick up an historical approach to their subject 'from the gutter,' as it were, then responsible folk must sit them down soon or later and tell them about it. Finding a way to do this, of course, is the great problem which every thoroughly modern economic historian must overcome. To paraphrase the advice in Thurber and White's manual: 'When imparting *sex* knowledge to one's *parents*, it is of the utmost importance to do it in such a way as not to engender fear or anxiety. Choose your phrasing carefully, explaining everything clearly while avoiding the use of terms that tend to cause nervousness in *older* people.'

So now for a short, matter-of-fact story. I have selected it with especial care, adhering to Thurber and White's recommendation to omit any allusions to birds and flowers, or other confusing biological analogies which economists are likely to take too literally and find upsetting.[2]

The Story of QWERTY

Why does the topmost row of letters on your personal computer keyboard spell out QWERTYUIOP, rather than something else? Nothing in the engineering of computer terminals requires the awkward keyboard layout known today as 'QWERTY.' The Maltron keyboard, developed by a British team, offers to save typists time and motion by dividing keys into more efficient groups: 91 per cent of the letters used most frequently in English are on the Maltron 'home row,' compared with 51 percent on the QWERTY keyboard. QWERTY forces your hands to 'hurdle,' that is to jump upwards or sideways so that fingers can strike keys, about 256 times more often than the Maltron arrangement whose tilted keyboard makes the letters easier to hit. But Maltron has arrived on the scene only recently, and we are all old enough to remember that QWERTY somehow had been passed down to us from the age of typewriters.

Clearly the computer manufacturers had not been persuaded by previous exhortations to discard QWERTY – even those which latter-day apostles of DSK (the Dvorak Simplified Keyboard) inserted in trade journals such as *Computers and Automation* during the early 1970s. Devotees of the keyboard arrangement patented in 1932 by August Dvorak and W. L. Dealey have long held most of the world's records for speed-typing. In the age of the manual typewriter the racing handicap imposed by QWERTY was especially heavy, except for those whose left hand and little fingers were uncommonly strong. Moreover, during the 1940's US Navy experiments had shown that the increased efficiency obtained with DSK would amortize the cost of retraining a group of typists within the first ten days of their subsequent full-time employment. Dvorak was a Professor of Education at the University of Washington in Seattle. He had lived his professional life as a disciple of Frank B. Gilbreth, the pioneer of time and motion studies and champion of the cause of designing 'machines for men not men for machines.' But he died, in 1975, a disappointed man. Had Dvorak construed Gilbreth's motto more literally and thought about the actual men and women who constituted the available supply of typists at the time, he might have spared himself the embittering frustration of the world's stubborn rejection of his contributions. As it was, his death came too soon for him to be solaced by the Apple IIC computer's built-in switch which

33

instantly converts its keyboard from QWERTY to virtual DSK, or to be further vexed by doubts that the switch would not often be flicked, and would remain more of a *curiosum* than a real selling point.

If as Apple advertising copy says, DSK 'lets you type 20–40% faster,' why did this superior design meet essentially the same resistance as the previous seven improvements on the QWERTY typewriter keyboard that were patented in the US and Britain during the years 1909–24? Was it the result of customary, non-rational behavior by countless individuals who had been socialized to carry on in an antiquated technological tradition? Or had there been a conspiracy among the members of the tyewriter oligopoly to suppress an invention which it was feared would, by increasing the productivity of each typist, ultimately curtail the demand for their machines? Dvorak himself once suggested that something like this lay at the root of the typewriter manufacturers' apparent disinterest in his patent. But perhaps we should turn instead to the other popular 'Devil Theory,' and ask if political regulation and interference with the workings of a 'free market' has been the cause of inefficient keyboard regimentation? Maybe it's all to be blamed on the public school system, like everything else that's awry?

Somehow you can already sense that these will not be the most promising lines along which to search for an economic understanding of QWERTY's present dominance. The agents engaged in production and purchase decisions in today's keyboard market are not the prisoners of custom, conspiracy, or state control. But while they are, as we now say, perfectly 'free to choose,' their behavior nevertheless is held fast in the grip of events long forgotten, and shaped by circumstances in which neither they nor their interests figured. Like the great men of whom Tolstoi wrote in *War and Peace* (Bk. IX,ch. 1), '(e)very action of theirs, that seems to them an act of their own free will, is in an historical sense not free at all, but in bondage to the whole course of previous history . . . .'

This is a short story, however. So it begins only little more than a century ago, with the fifty-second man to invent the typewriter. Christopher Latham Sholes was a printer by trade and mechanical tinkerer by inclination. Helped by his friends Carlos Glidden and Samuel W. Soule, who also spent much of their time hanging around C. F. Kleinsteuber's machine shop on the northern edge of Milwaukee, Wisconsin during the 1860s, he had built a primitive writing machine for which a patent application was filed in October 1867. Many defects in the working of Sholes' 'Type Writer' stood in the way of its immediate commercial introduction. Because the printing point was located underneath the paper-carriage, it was quite invisible to the operator. 'Non-visibility' remained an unfortunate feature for this and other up-stroke machines long after the flat paper carriage of the original design had been supplanted by arrangements closely resembling the modern continuous roller-platen. Consequently, the tendency of the typebars to clash and jam if struck in rapid succession was a particularly serious defect. When a typebar would stick at or near the printing point, every succeeding stroke would merely serve to hammer the same impression onto the paper. But the resulting string of repeated letters would be discovered only at the end of the paragraph, or whenever the typist bothered to raise the carriage to inspect what had been printed. Unsticking jammed typebars was a correspondingly awkward and time-consuming maneuvre, compared to which the jumps and slips of the weight-driven carriage escapement mechanism, or the tendency of the weight itself to come loose and crash onto the operator's foot, were merely secondary annoyances.

Urged onward by the bullying optimism of James Densmore, the promoter-venture capitalist whom he had taken into the partnership in 1867, Sholes struggled for the next six years to perfect 'the machine.' It was during this painful interval that a four-row, upper case keyboard approaching the modern QWERTY standard emerged, from the inventor's trial-and-error rearrangement of the original model's alphabetical key ordering in an effort to reduce the frequency of typebar clashes. Vestiges of the primordial layout remained, as they do to this day in the 'home row' sequence: FGHJKL, with 'I' close by in the second row. In March, 1873 Densmore, with the help of a smooth-talking salesman who went by the name of George Washington Yost, succeeded in placing the manufacturing rights for the substantially transformed Sholes–Glidden 'Type Writer' with E. Remington and Sons, the famous arms makers. Within the next few months QWERTY's evolution was virtually completed by Remington's mechanics, William Jenne and Jefferson Clough. Their many modifications included some fine-tuning of the keyboard design in the course of which the 'R' wound up in the place previously allotted to the period mark '.'.

QWERTY thus had evolved primarily as the chance solution to an engineering design problem in the construction of a typewriter which would work reliably at a rate significantly faster than a copyist could write. Marketing considerations also may have played some role in Jenne and Clough's final keyboard shuffles; it has been suggested that the main advantage of putting the R into QWERTY was that it thereby gathered into one row all the letters which a salesman would need, to impress customers by rapidly pecking out the brand name: TYPE WRITER

Nevertheless, the early commercial fortunes of the machine with which QWERTY's destiny had become linked remained extremely precarious. The economic downturn of the 1870s was not the best of times in which to be selling Americans a novel piece of office equipment costing $125 apiece. When the Depression lifted, early in the 1880s, Remington's sales of the Improved Model Two (introduced, complete with recently patented carriage shift key, in 1878) began to pick up pace; annual typewriter production reached the rate of 1200 units in 1881. But the market position which QWERTY had acquired during the course of its early career was far from deeply entrenched; the entire stock of QWERTY-embodying machines in the US could not have much exceeded 5000 when the decade opened.

Its future also was not much protected by any compelling technological necessities. For there were ways to make a typewriter without the up-stroke typebar mechanism that had called forth the QWERTY adaptation, and rival designs were appearing on the American scene – not to mention those already established in Europe. A down-stroke design with an 'almost visible' printing point would be patented by Charles Spiro and introduced in New York as the 'Bar-Lock' typewriter in 1889, to be followed a year later by the first fully visible down-stroke machine, manufactured by the Daugherty Typewriter Co. of Pennsylvania. By 1893 Francis X. Wagner's superior design for a front-stroke visible machine with a four-row keyboard was patented, and in another three years it would be taken over by John Underwood's typewriter-supply firm to become the prototype for all the following upright front-stroke machines. Front-stroke action and visibility would greatly mitigate the problems of typebar jamming which were the original rationale for QWERTY's existence.

Meanwhile, back in 1878 when Remington had just brought out the Model Two and the whole enterprise was teetering on the edge of bankruptcy, the print-wheel offered a more radical but immediately available alternative to the typebar technology. It had been used in the Englishman John Pratt's typewriter of 1866, the fateful description of which, in the magazine *Scientific American*, had been shown to our hero Sholes during the following year by his friend Glidden. Furthermore, a patent had been filed for an electric print-wheel device in 1872 by a young mechanic at the Automatic Telegraph Co. in New York. This was none other than Thomas Edison, who, having helped improve one of the many Sholes–Glidden experimental models around 1870, then set out to prove that he could build a better instrument for printing telegraphs than the machine which Densmore and Sholes were urging upon his employers. This particular Edison invention went on to be used in teletype machines, leaving the instrument introduced in 1879 by a former Remington employee, Lucien Stephen Crandall, the honor of being the second typewriter to reach the US market. It was also the first commercial entrant that circumvented the problem of clashing typebars by dispensing with them entirely, in favor of an arrangement of the type on a cylindrical sleeve. The sleeve was made to revolve to the required letter and come down onto the printing point, locking in place for correct alignment. So much for the 'revolutionary' character of the IBM 72/82's 'golfball' design.

Very soon thereafter, in 1881, the first units of James Bartlett Hammond's alternative to the typebar system entered the American market using a swinging type-sector to insure perfect alignment and a rubber buffered hammer located behind the paper to achieve evenness of impression. While Hammond's first model was offered with a curved two-row keyboard, with the introduction of his Model Two in 1893 a square three-row layout also became available. Freed from the legacy of typebars, the arrangement of keys offered by the Hammond from the outset was more sensible than QWERTY: its so-called 'ideal' keyboard placed the sequence DHIATENSOR in the home row, these being ten letters with which one may compose over 70 percent of the words in the English language. The same, ideal layout later appeared on the small type-wheel portable with a three-row keyboard and double shift, first patented in 1889 and marketed as the Model Five by the Blickensderfer Manufacturing Company in 1893. (Notice that Dvorak also used these ten letters in his keyboard's home row, AOEUIDHTNS, except for the replacement of the R with U.)

The beginning of the typewriter boom in the 1880s had thus witnessed a rapid proliferation of competitive designs, manufacturing companies and keyboard arrangements rivalling the Sholes–Remington QWERTY. Yet, by the middle of the next decade, just when it had become evident that any micro-technological rationale for QWERTY's dominance was being removed by the progress of typewriter engineering, the US industry was rapidly moving toward the standard of an upright front-stroke machine with a four-row QWERTY keyboard that was referred to as 'The Universal.' The authorities disagree as to the exact dating, but it appears that sometime around 1896 George Blickensderfer started to offer 'The Universal' as an optional alternative to the Ideal keyboard on the various machines in the illustrious 'Blick' line. Hammond too seems to have fallen into step, offering the same option at least by 1905.

Basic QWERTY-nomics

To understand what had happened in this fateful interval, the economist must attend to the fact that typewriters were beginning to take their place as an element of a larger, rather complex system of production that was technically interrelated. This system involved typewriter operators as well as typewriting machines, and therefore the relevant decision agents within it included others besides the makers and buyers of typewriter hardware: there were the typists who supplied a skilled labor service to employers, and the variety of organizations, both private and public, undertaking to train people in such skills. Still more critical to the outcome was the fact that, in contrast to the hardware subsystems of which QWERTY or other keyboards were a part, this larger system of production was nobody's design. It was not conceived at the outset, in the dreams of Sholes, Glidden, Densmore or Philo Remington. Rather like the proverbial Topsy, and much else in the history of economics besides, it 'jes' growed.'

Instruction in typewriters began to be offered by private business colleges in New York City soon after the first Remington-built machines became available, but emphasis was placed upon mastering the mechanical operations rather than typing *per se*. In 1880 the firm of N. T. Underwood issued one of the earliest instructional handbooks containing 'inductive exercises, arranged with a typical guide to correct use of the fingers;' only some of the fingers, however. It was not until 1882 that the radical innovation of an eight-finger typing method was put forward by the proprietress of Longley's Shorthand and Typewriter Institute, in Cincinnati. Her pamphlet happened to be 'adapted to Remington's perfected typewriters.' That very same year, the New York firm of Wyckoff, Seamans & Benedict, having just bought the worldwide sales agency rights for the Remington Type Writer from the firm of E. Remington & Sons, began to promote their product by imitating another instructional innovation that lately had been introduced by the City's Central Branch of the YWCA. The 'Y' had organized an experimental class to teach eight young women to typewrite during 1881 and, despite critics' predictions that typewriting was destined to remain a masculine occupation, every one of the female graduates had found employment quickly. Remington schools for typewriting soon joined the private business and stenographic 'colleges' that were now springing up in all the leading cities.

But Mrs L. V. Longley's *Typewriter Lessons* were not sufficient to carry the day immediately for the proponents of eight-finger typing. She was denounced repeatedly in the pages of *Cosmopolitan Shorthander* and eventually was challenged to prove her case by another teacher of typewriting from her own city. The challenger, one Louis Taub, proclaimed the superiority of four-finger typing on the Caligraph. This was a rival machine which had been brought out in 1881 by Densmore's former partner, Yost. It came equipped with a six-row keyboard, accommodating upper- and lower-case keys to make up for its lack of the Remington's shift-action. In 1888, when the first public speed-typing competition was organized which put to the test these contending systems, the honor of Mrs Longley and the Remington was vindicated by a Federal Court stenographer from Salt Lake City who had taught himself to type on a Remington No. 1, way back in 1878. Frank E.

McGurrin, the man who entered the lists as their champion against Louis Taub, already had won fame in demonstrations before gasping audiences throughout the West, because, in addition to deploying the 'all-finger' technique, he had memorized the QWERTY keyboard. We shall never know whether he could have managed the same feat with the 72 keys of the Caligraph machine.

The advent of 'touch' typing, the name coined for McGurrin's method in a manual of typewriter instructions published in 1889, gave rise to three features of the evolving production system that were crucially important in causing QWERTY to become 'locked in' as the dominant keyboard arrangement. These were *technical interrelatedness*, *economies of scale* and *quasi-irreversibility* of investment. They constitute the basic ingredients of what might be called 'QWERTY-nomics.'

Technical interrelatedness, or the need for system compatibility between keyboard 'hardware' and the 'software' represented by the touch-typist's memory of a particular arrangement of the keys, meant that the expected present value of a typewriter as an instrument of production was dependent upon the availability of compatible 'software' created by typists' decisions as to the kind of keyboard they should learn. Prior to the growth of the personal market for typewriters the purchasers of the hardware typically were business firms, and therefore distinct from the owners of typing skills. Few incentives existed at the time, or later, for any one business to invest in providing its employees with a form of general human capital which so readily could be taken elsewhere. (Notice that it was the wartime US Navy, not your typical employer, who undertook the experiment of retraining typists on the Dvorak keyboard.) The investment decisions of would-be touch typists, and the consequent supply of clerical and office workers with those skills, therefore remained largely beyond the individual control of the buyers in the market for typewriter hardware. Nevertheless, the purchase by a potential employer of a QWERTY keyboard conveyed a positive pecuniary

41

externality to compatibly trained touch-typists. To the degree to which this increased the likelihood that subsequent typists would choose to learn QWERTY in preference to another method for which the stock of compatible hardware would not be so large, the overall user costs of a typewriting system based upon QWERTY (or any specific keyboard) would tend to *decrease* as it gained in acceptance relative to other systems. Essentially symmetrical conditions obtained in the market for instruction in touch-typing. There, typists' decisions to learn the QWERTY keyboard would raise the value of QWERTY-equipped machines to their employer-owners. By increasing the likelihood that such machines would be installed in preference to others, such a decision raised the probability that another prospective typist subsequently would opt to be trained in a QWERTY-based method.

These decreasing cost conditions – or *system scale economies* – had a number of consequences, among which undoubtedly the most important was the tendency for the process of inter-system competition to lead toward *de facto* standardization through the predominance of a single keyboard design. For analytical purposes, the matter can be simplified by supposing that buyers of typewriters uniformly were without inherent preferences concerning keyboards, and cared only about how the stock of touch-typists was distributed among alternative specific keyboard styles. The candidates for typewriter instruction, on the other hand, may be supposed to have been heterogeneous in their preferences for learning QWERTY-based 'touch', as opposed to other methods, but attentive also to the way the stock of machines was distributed according to keyboard styles. If we imagine the members of this hetero-geneous population deciding in random order what kind of typing training to acquire, it may be seen that with unbounded decreasing costs of selection each stochastic decision in favor of QWERTY would raise the probability (but not guarantee) that the next selector would favor QWERTY. From the viewpoint of the formal theory of stochastic processes, what we are looking at now is equivalent to a generalized 'Polya urn scheme.' In a simple scheme of that kind, an urn containing balls of various colors is sampled with replacement and every drawing of a ball of a specified color results in a second ball of the same color being returned to the urn; the probabilities that balls of specified colors will be added are therefore increasing (linear) functions of the proportions in which the respective colors are represented within the urn. A recent theorem due to Arthur, Ermoliev and Kaniovski[3] allows us to say that when generalized forms of such processes (characterized by increasing returns) are extended indefinitely, the selection probabilities eventually approach a limit function (if one exists) and the proportional share of one of the colors will, with probability one, converge to unity.

There may be many eligible candidates for supremacy, and from an *ex ante* vantage point we cannot say with corresponding certainty which among the contending colors – or rival keyboard arrangements – will be the one to gain eventual dominance. That part of the story is likely to be governed by 'historical accidents,' which is to say, by the particular sequencing of choices made close to the beginnings of the process. It is there that essentially random, transient factors are most likely to exert great leverage, as has been neatly shown by Arthur's model[4] of the dynamics of technological competition under increasing returns.

Intuition suggests that if choices were made in a forward-looking way, rather than myopically on the basis of comparisons among the currently prevailing costs of different systems, the final outcome could be influenced strongly by the expectations that investors in system components – whether specific touch-typing skills or typewriters – came to hold regarding the decisions that would be made by the other agents. A particular system could triumph over rivals merely because the purchasers of the software (and/or the hardware) expected that it would do so. This intuition seems to be supported by recent formal analyses of markets where purchasers of rival products benefit from externalities conditional upon the size of the compatible system or 'network' with which they thereby become joined: Katz and Shapiro[5] and Hanson[6] have recently demonstrated the crucial role played by expectations in both static and dynamic duopoly games of this kind respectively. Thus, although the early lead acquired by QWERTY through its initial association with the Remington was quantitatively very slender, when magnified by expectations it may well have been quite sufficient to guarantee that the industry eventually would lock in to a *de facto* QWERTY standard.

The occurrence of this 'lock in' as early as the mid 1890s does appear to have owed something also to other causes. Conventional *economies of scale* were part of the story, as these soon were exploited by the private business colleges that taught young men and women to touch-type through the use of instruction manuals. Those organizations' impact upon the supply of QWERTY-habituated typists remained minor by comparison with the public high school systems that at a much later point, in the 1920s, began to include typewriting among their expanding curriculum of 'business' subjects. Nevertheless, the activities of business and commercial colleges offering stenography and typewriting during the late 1880s and early 1890s brought them into contact with both prospective employers and typewriter companies' sales agencies. Considerable leverage was thereby given to the numerically tiny cadre of pioneer touch-typing teachers who had become habituated to using the QWERTY keyboard.

The strategic significance of this latter point is brought out more fully by considering the third critical element among those I enumerated as having been added by the innovation of touch-typing. This was the high costs of 'software conversion', and the consequent *quasi-irreversibility of investment* in labor force training. The human capital formed in learning to touch-type is remarkably durable, for the skill resembles that of bicycle-riding or swimming in that once mastered it is long retained at some functional level and may be upgraded rapidly

44

by practice. Moreover, once a specific touch-typing program has been 'installed in memory' it becomes quite costly (in retraining time and typing errors) to convert the afflicted typist to a different program. Thus, as far as keyboard conversion costs were concerned, an important asymmetry had appeared between the software and the hardware components of the evolving typewriting system: the costs of typewriter software conversion were going up, whereas the costs of typewriter hardware conversion were coming down. While the novel, non-typebar technologies developed during the 1880s were freeing the keyboard from technical bondage to QWERTY, by the same token typewriter makers were freed from fixed-cost bondage to any particular keyboard arrangement. Manufacturers who adopted those engineering advances found it very inexpensive to provide the QWERTY option to any customers who might prefer it to the other keyboards they were being offered. A market inducement for producers to standardize voluntarily, at least in this one attribute, had arisen with the demonstrated superiority of QWERTY-based touch-typing over the four-finger hunt-and-peck method. Curiously, no public trial seems to have been held during the 1890s to determine whether or not a hunt-and-peck typist using the more efficient, Ideal keyboard also could be bested by the likes of Frank McGurrin (using QWERTY). But it is not clear whether the outcome would have mattered at all by that time.

It was enough that non-QWERTY typewriter manufacturers could switch cheaply to achieve compatibility with the QWERTY-programmed typists, who could not. For a producer newly entering the typewriter market the short-run attractions surely lay in the direction of expanding market share quickly. And this would mean catering to the needs of the extant 'installed base' of QWERTY-programmed typists, though it must still have been quite small even a decade after McGurrin's 1888 victory over Taub. My own estimates for 1900, based on a sampling of the manuscript schedules of the US Census in that year, indicate that there were some 8200–9200 gainfully occupied typists ('type-writers,' they were called) in the country, of whom at least 5500 had entered the pursuit during the preceding ten years when QWERTY-based touch-typing was coming into vogue. Since at this time American women typically left the workforce at marriage, and the mean age at marriage was declining among the white native born who dominated the ranks of female office workers, the potential personal typewriter market represented by the stock of QWERTY-trained typists must have struck contemporary observers as considerably larger and expanding steadily. This, then, was a situation in which the precise details of timing had made it privately profitable in the short run to adapt machines to men (or, as was the case increasingly, to women) rather than the other way around. And the business has continued that way ever since.

Message

In place of a moral, I want to leave you with a message of faith and qualified hope. The story of QWERTY is a rather intriguing one for economists. Despite the presence of the sort of externalities that standard static analysis tells us would interfere with the achievement of the socially optimal degree of system compatibility, competition in the absence of perfect futures markets drove the industry prematurely into *de facto* standardization *on the wrong system* – and that is where decentralized decision-making subsequently has sufficed to hold it. Outcomes of this kind are not so exotic. For such things to happen seems only too possible in the presence of strong technical interrelatedness, scale economies, and irreversibilities due to learning and habituation. They come as no surprise to readers prepared by Thorstein Veblen's classic passages in *Germany and the Industrial Revolution*[7], on the problem of Britain's under-sized railway wagons and 'the penalties of taking the lead;' they may be painfully familiar to students who have been obliged to assimilate the details of deservedly less renowned scribblings of mine[8] about the obstacles which ridge-and-furrow placed in the path of British farm mechanization, or the influence of remote events in nineteenth-century US factor price history upon the subsequently emerging bias towards Hicksian labor-saving improvements in the production technology set for certain branches of manufacturing.

I believe there are many more QWERTY worlds lying out there in the past, on the very edges of the modern economic analyst's tidy universe; worlds we do not yet fully perceive or understand, but whose influence, like that of dark stars, extends none the less to shape the visible orbits of our contemporary economic affairs. Most of the time I feel sure that the absorbing delights and quiet terrors of exploring QWERTY worlds will suffice to draw adventurous economists into the systematic study of essentially *historical* dynamic processes, and so will seduce them into the ways of economic history and a better grasp of their own subject matter.

But will it? Messrs Thurber and White[9] concluded their chapter with a gentle warning not to bet too heavily on the passive approach to educating a parent, along these lines: 'Sometimes it may be advisable to quote to your *parents* directly from standard works on the subject of *sex*. When this is felt to be too abrupt, less intrusive approaches may seem attractive. Some *children* have told me that instead of quoting from books they have left the books lying around, opened at pertinent pages. But even this has failed to work in most cases. A book that is lying around soon will seem dusty to the average *parent*. The "mothers" will usually pick it up, dust it, and close it.'

Notes

1   James Thurber and E. B. White, *Is Sex Necessary? or Why You Feel the Way You Do*, Garden City, New York: Blue Ribbon Books, 1929.
2   What follows is an expanded version of the text that was published under the title 'Clio and the Economics of QWERTY' in *The American Economic*

Review, Papers and Proceedings, vol. 75, no. 2 (May, 1985), pp. 332–7. It does not reflect the voluminous correspondence I received subsequent to the Dallas, Texas Meetings of the A.E.A., on the subject of typewriters, their keyboards, other illustrations of path-dependent dynamic processes, and their mathematical representations. I am grateful for the support that the limited piece of research, reported on here, received under a grant to the Technological Innovation Program of the Center for Economic Policy Research, Stanford University. Douglas Puffert supplied able research assistance. The text and references record some but not the whole of my indebtedness to Brian Arthur's views on QWERTY and QWERTY-like subjects. I bear full responsibility, naturally, for errors of fact and interpretation, as well as for the peculiar opinions on the necessity of history (and sex) represented in these pages.

3   W. Brian Arthur, Yuri M. Ermoliev and Yuri M. Kanlovski, 'On Generalized Urn Schemes of the Polya Kind,' *Kibernetika*, vol. 19, no. 1, (1983), pp. 49–56, translated from the Russian in *Cybernetics*, vol. 19 (1983), pp. 61–71. W. Brian Arthur, Yuri M. Ermoliev and Yuri M. Kaniovski, 'Strong Laws for a Class of Path-Dependent Urn Processes,' in *Proceedings of the International Conference on Stochastic Optimization, Kiev 1984*, Berlin: Springer Verlag, 1985.

4   W. Brian Arthur, 'On Competing Technologies and Historical Small Events: The Dynamics of Choice Under Increasing Returns,' *Technological Innovation Program Workshop Paper*, Department of Economics, Stanford University, November 1983, 31 pp.

5   Michael L. Katz and Carl Shapiro, 'Network Externalities, Competition, and Compatibility,' *Woodrow Wilson School Discussion in Economics No. 54*, Princeton University, September, 1983, 34 pp.

6   Ward A. Hanson, 'Bandwagons and Orphans: Dynamic Pricing of Competing Technological Systems Subject to Decreasing Costs,' *Technological Innovation Program Workshop Paper*, Department of Economics, Stanford University, January 1984, 34 pp.

7   Thorstein Veblen, *Imperial Germany and the Industrial Revolution*, New York: Macmillan 1915, esp. pp. 126–27.

8   Paul A. David, *Technical choice, innovation and economic growth: Essays on American and British experience in the nineteenth century*, New York: Cambridge University Press, 1975, ch. 1. Paul A. David 'The Landscape and the Machine: Technical Interrelatedness, Land Tenure and the Mechanization of the Corn Harvest in Victorian Britain.' In *Essays on a Mature Economy: Britain after 1840*, ch. 5, ed. D.N. McCloskey, London: Methuen, 1971.

9   James Thurber and E.B. White, *Is Sex Necessary?*, ch. 6.

Bibliography

Adler, Michael M., *The Writing Machine*, London: George Allen & Unwin Ltd., 1973.

Baker, Elizabeth F., *Technology and Women's Work*, New York: Columbia University Press, 1964, esp. pp.70–4.

Beeching, Wilfred A., *The Century of the Typewriter*, New York: St Martin's Press, 1974.

Bliven, Bruce, *The Wonderful Writing Machine*, New York: Random House, 1954.

Davies, Margery W., *Women's Place is at the Typewriter: Office Work and Office Workers, 1870–1930*, Philadelphia: Temple University Press, 1982, esp. pp. 51–78.

Dvorak, August, Nellie L. Merrick, William L. Dealey and Gertrude C. Ford, *Typewriting Behavior*, New York: American Book Company, 1936.

Edwards, Alba M., *Comparative Occupational Statistics for the United States, 1870 to 1940*, Part of the Sixteenth Census of the United States: 1940, Washington, DC: Government Printing Office, 1943.

Graham, Stephen N., *1900 Public Use Sample: User's Handbook*, Center for Studies in Demography and Ecology, University of Washington, Seattle, July 1980.

Haynes, Benjamin R. and Harry P. Jackson, *A History of Business Education in the United States*, San Francisco: South-Western Publishing Co., 1935, esp. pp.28–71.

Knepper, Edwin G., *History of Business Education in United States*, Bowling Green, Ohio, 1941, esp. pp. 73–94, 125–48.

Robert Parkinson, 'The Dvorak Simplified Keyboard: Forty Years of Frustration.' *Computers and Automation* (November 1972), pp.18–25.

Time Magazine, 'The Case of QWERTY vs. Maltron' (January 26, 1981), p. 35.

5

Is History Stranger than Theory?
The Origin of Telephone Separations

PETER TEMIN

In order to illustrate the interaction between economic theory and economic history, I have chosen to analyze a very recent historical episode. The contemporaneous nature of this event is used to argue that history is a matter of methodology, not of dates: current events as well as medieval ones can be seen historically.

This event is suitable for this symposium because the existing theoretical and historical analyses reach different, conflicting conclusions. But resolution of this conflict does not involve a contest between history and theory. Careful historical analysis reveals that the historical and theoretical analyses in question were performed on the basis of quite different underlying conceptions of the world. It is no accident that they reached opposite conclusions. Review of the historical analysis shows both that the accepted history expressed a particular point of view and that the received theory omitted important aspects of the events under examination. But before commenting on this state of affairs, let us examine the history so as to expose and resolve the conflict.

The integrated Bell Telephone System that we all grew up with vanished on January 1, 1984, to be replaced by a new, more open telephone network still in the process of definition.

This research was supported by a grant from the AT&T. All interpretations and conclusions are mine alone.

50

AT&T's divestiture of the telephone operating companies resulted from the settlement of an antitrust suit against AT&T begun in 1974 and carried forward under three Administrations in Washington. The trial was conducted in 1981, largely under the direction of William Baxter, the first Assistant Attorney General for Antitrust in the Reagan Administration, and the settlement was negotiated by him and the management of AT&T.

Baxter articulated his theory of the case to Senator Thurmond's Judiciary Committee midway through the AT&T trial. He said, among other things, 'If one argues for divestiture, one argues that the cross-subsidy problem is terribly important, that the vertical integration economies probably are not very great, and that regulatory supervision is unwanted and more deregulation is possible.'[1] Divestiture, in other words, would solve 'the cross-subsidy problem' without doing much violence to the telephone network. But what is 'the cross-subsidy problem?' The government's economics experts in the antitrust suit asserted that AT&T's integrated structure gave it the opportunity and the incentive to subsidize its competitive long-distance services with revenues from its regulated local monopolies.[2] This, presumably, was one of the antitrust violations on which the government's suit was based. It is entirely in accord with the lines of the negotiated divestiture. And as expressed by the government economics experts, it was a theoretical proposition deriving from the existence of local monopoly and a competition in the long-distance service. The prosecutor in the case had said the opposite to the Senate Judiciary Committee: 'AT&T has subsidized local telephone service with long line revenues.' This pattern, he said, was probably continuing at the time of his appearance before the committee.[3] Baxter's historical observation, in other words, contradicted the witnesses' theoretical assertion. Confusion on this scale cries for explanation. The explanation demonstrates the need for historical as well as theoretical analysis.

A little terminology will facilitate the historical narrative. A telephone 'station' is what we colloquially refer to as a telephone. A toll 'board' is the local exchange switch which routes local calls within the exchange and toll calls out of the exchange. There are two distinct models of telephone communication which have given rise to two different modes of accounting. In station-to-station accounting, a long-distance call is thought of as going from one telephone (station) to another. In the board-to-board model, the same call is broken into parts. The parts between the individual stations and their local exchanges (boards) are considered local; the long-distance call goes only between the local exchanges, that is, from board to board.

AT&T established its first toll rate schedule in 1889, the rates becoming applicable as service was opened. AT&T established its accounting on a board-to-board basis, reflecting its initial conception of telephone communication as it developed from local companies, linked into a national network by its overarching corporate organization.[4]

During the First World War the Postmaster General operated the telephone system. Not subject to the jurisdictional limitations that would later separate state and federal regulatory authorities, he set uniform interstate and intrastate toll rates and these remained in effect through 1926, when AT&T instituted an interstate rate reduction. The FCC negotiated four additional reductions in interstate telephone rates before the Second World War, although it did not try to compute returns separately on the companies' interstate and intrastate assets as a part of these rate negotiations. But in 1923, Illinois Bell had contested a rate reduction ordered by the Illinois Commerce Commission and the case reached the US Supreme Court as *Smith v. Illinois Bell*. The Supreme Court ruled that the issue of whether the mandated rates were 'confiscatory' under the Fourteenth Amendment could not be decided without 'specific findings' on the allocation of Illinois Bell's assets between interstate and intrastate service. Referring to the 'indisputable fact' that 'exchange property' is used both for intrastate and interstate service, the Court said that, 'It is obvious that, unless an apportionment is made, the intrastate service to which the exchange property is allocated will bear an undue burden – to what extent is a matter of controversy.'[5] In other words, the 'specific findings' needed to determine whether rates were confiscatory were to be based on station-to-station accounting, while intrastate telephone rates were to be set high enough to earn a satisfactory return on the capital allocated to intrastate service and so under state jurisdiction.

These issues arose in various states in the 1930s. Then during the Second World War when wartime traffic raised Long Lines' profits above the allowed level, the FCC began to examine the division of assets between interstate and intrastate activities. The Commission needed both to reduce Long Lines' profits and to respond to the federal government's wartime demands on the interstate telephone network; and the Commission was acutely aware of the concerns of state regulators as to the differentials between interstate and intrastate rates for telephone calls over comparable distances. As interstate rates declined, comparable toll calls within states came to cost more than calls crossing state lines.[6]

The traditional way of reducing Long Lines' 'excessive' profits, i.e. by reducing interstate rates, was doubly problematical: it would increase the disparity between interstate and intrastate toll rates and also raise the quantity of interstate toll service demanded by the non-military public. The FCC therefore sought to reduce Long Lines' profits by moving some expenses of local telephone services into interstate jurisdiction, that is, by using station-to-station accounting. Agreement on the use of separations procedures that divided expenses along station-to-station lines was reached in a series of meetings between representatives of AT&T and several FCC Commissioners in January, 1943.[7]

The wartime agreement on separations procedures was embodied in the 1947 *Manual of Separations*. The FCC refrained from endorsing the manual, but said it would not object to its use. Telephone rates were set on the basis that exchange capital not sensitive to the volume of traffic was allocated to interstate toll service according to the relative use of telephones as measured by the 'subscriber line use' or SLU, where

SLU = (minutes of interstate use)/(total minutes of use).

AT&T's acceptance of the new accounting and separations procedures undoubtedly was based on its appreciation of the changed regulatory environment arising from the establishment of the FCC. Before 1934, the interstate telephone service was essentially unregulated, and it made sense to keep expenses in state jurisdiction and revenues out of it. As the FCC gained influence and AT&T's allowable interstate rate of return declined, AT&T lost the incentive to keep its rate base in state jurisdiction. AT&T therefore acceded to the federal government's wartime needs and the state regulators' need for toll-rate uniformity. (After all, the structure of telephone rates was not a major issue in a unitary system.) It agreed to base rates on station-to-station accounting, but it preserved its internal board-to-board accounting, using separations procedures to convert the figures from one model to the other.

In response to a 1950 FCC inquiry into interstate rates, AT&T proposed an alteration of the 1947 *Manual of Separations* that would have shifted more of the local telephone plant into the interstate rate base and avoided or moderated a fall in interstate rates. The national organization of state regulatory commissioners, NARUC, strongly supported the plan since it provided the opportunity to reduce intrastate rates. The FCC, however, rejected it as inconsistent with *Smith v. Illinois Bell* since 'its adoption would have the effect of introducing an arbitrary method whereby interstate services subject to Federal jurisdiction would, in effect, be subsidizing services beyond that jurisdiction.' The FCC seems to have argued that SLU was the 'correct' way to allocate costs between local and toll services.

The National Association of Railroad and Utility Commissioners (NARUC) sought redress through Senator Earnest W.
McFarland of Arizona, the Republican majority leader and
chairman of the Communications Subcommittee of the Senate
Interstate Commerce Committee. It appealed to him at its
1950 convention held in the senator's home state. He responded
with a letter to the FCC in which he expressed his dismay at the
commission's apparent willingness to 'shift the load from the
big user to the little user; from the large national corporations
which are heavy users of long distance to the average
housewife and business or professional man who do not
indulge in a great deal of long distance.' Noting the growing
disparity between interstate and intrastate toll rates for
comparable calls, the senator said, 'I am not in a position to
pass upon the question as to whether the remedy suggested by
NARUC is the proper one but I am certain that something
should be done – and at once.'

The FCC either misjudged or ignored the intent of Senator
McFarland's letter in its reply. It sent him a long summary of
the history of separations replete with facts and figures in
which it characterized the disparity in toll rates as 'natural' and
asserted that it was fulfilling its legal mandate to regulate
interstate rates only. Senator McFarland replied sharply: 'I
believe that the Commission's six-page reply takes a strictly
technical attitude toward the whole problem rather than the
broad, constructive viewpoint required by the Communications
Act . . . Frankly, the Commission's reply is disappointing to
me and to my colleagues whose interest and concern occasioned
my original letter to you.'

The FCC promptly reopened negotiations with AT&T. A
revision of separations procedures resulted that shifted enough
capital to interstate operations to justify two interstate rate
increases, in the next two years. These were the first interstate
rate increases granted since the FCC was created. They also
took place at a time when technological changes were reducing
the cost of long-distance service. The toll rate disparity to

which Senator McFarland had directed the FCC's attention was sharply reduced. The FCC stipulated cost allocations by which, on its own admission, long-distance revenues were used to subsidize local service.

When Long Lines' earnings rose in 1955, the FCC negotiated another revision of the 1947 *Manual* that followed the lines of the plan rejected by the FCC five years earlier. The new revision shifted even more capital into interstate jurisdiction. A series of further revisions continued the process of shifting exchange plant into the interstate arena, demonstrating the lasting imprint of the agreement between Congress, state and federal regulators and AT&T which was reached in the early 1950s.

The issue of accounting models arose again in the 1960s and 1970s in reference to different problems and clothed in different language. As potential competitors appealed to the FCC for access to parts of the interstate telephone market, the FCC became concerned about cross-subsidization *among* interstate services. The ensuing debate about cost allocation between various Bell services pitted the two theories against one another. The FCC opted for a system based on fully distributed cost, where joint costs are allocated to different services according to relative use, as measured by an analogue of SLU. This was station-to-station accounting under a more modern name. AT&T favored the use of long-run incremental costs, i.e. the additional long-run costs from adding any particular interstate service. This was an equally clear extension of the board-to-board model of long-distance service. The FCC rejected the use of long-run incremental costs as too subjective, but the preceding discussion of separations shows that the actual use of fully distributed costs is no less arbitrary and equally subject to manipulation.[8]

The divestiture also raised the question of accounting models, albeit implicitly, since the telephone network was split up along board-to-board lines. AT&T and other interexchange carriers furnish board-to-board long-distance service, now called interLATA service, while the Regional Holding Companies and their operating companies supply local (intraLATA) service. While some Cassandras saw the immediate end of separations procedures and consequent steep rises in local rates, Congress was up in arms over this now traditional issue, and the FCC has – so far – fallen once again into line. Current controversies over access charges preserve in new form the old disputes over accounting models.

Where, then, does the current confusion over cross-subsidies come from? Only under the board-to-board model is there a clear subsidy from long-distance to local service. And, as has been shown here, the FCC has rejected the use of that model for forty years. Using a game-theoretic definition,[9] Peters and I have shown that there can be no cross-subsidy from long-distance to local service under station-to-station accounting. There *can* be a subsidy from local service to long-distance service in the station-to-station model, but only if the costs of local service in isolation are even *less* than their current costs minus separations payments. In other words, there is a clear subsidy in one direction under the board-to-board model, and there *may be* a subsidy in the other direction under the station-to-station model.[10] Even though divestiture has brought board-to-board accounting out of the closet once again, it has not clarified the difference between the two accounting models.

Let us return then to our original paradox. Baxter clearly was using the board-to-board model in his Congressional testimony. Separations payments in that model are a cross-subsidy to local service. His economic expert witnesses, by contrast, were using a station-to-station model in which the costs of long-distance service was thought to be even *larger* than those implied by current separations payments and related financial flows within AT&T. No evidence was given in court on the magnitudes involved in this application of the station-to-station model, making the conclusion hard to evaluate. Lacking such an evaluation, there seems to be little evidence of a cross-subsidy to interstate long-distance services under either model.

Why does the confusion still exist? Is it just confusion stemming from inadequate analysis? Or does it serve larger purposes? Was it, possibly, a factor in the break-up of the AT&T? Instead of grappling with these important questions in this small space, let us return to the question of the relation of history to theory.

The need for historical analysis to clarify the relation between theory and observation should be clear. The predictions of economic theory may fail to express historical reality for many reasons. In this case, the model of a profit-maximizing firm was used without adequate attention to the political constraints on the firm's behavior. And the historical record also may be confused to the point where it is unclear which predictions have been fulfilled. Careful historical analysis can be avoided only at the economist's peril.

It goes almost without saying that responsible economic history needs to be informed by economic theory. Theory guides and focuses the historical inquiry; and the historical account may also stimulate questions for economic theory. How is it possible that a clearly identified confusion over accounting models could persist for decades and show up in a critically important antitrust suit without resolution? I am willing to hazard historical explanations; I hope that professional theorists will see this question also as a challenge for economic theory.

Notes

1 William J. Baxter, 'Testimony,' U.S. Senate, Committee on the Judiciary, 97th Congress, 1st Session, Hearings, 'DOJ Oversight: U.S. v. AT&T,' August 6, 1981, p. 27.
2 Bruce W. Owen, 'Testimony,' *U.S. v. AT&T Co.*, June 22, 1981. Nina W. Cornell, 'Testimony', *U.S. v. AT&T Co.*, June 19, 1981.
3 William J. Baxter, 'Testimony', 1981, p. 37.
4 Federal Communications Commission (FCC), *Investigation of the Telephone Industry in the United Staes, 1939*, New York: Arno Press, 1974, pp. 370–5.

5 *Smith v. Illinois Bell Telephone Co.*, 282 U.S. 133 (1930), p. 151.
6 National Assocation of Railroad and Utilities Commissioners (NARUC) and Federal Communications Commission (FCC), Telephone Toll Rates Subcommittee. *Message Toll Telephone Rates and Disparities*, Washington, DC, 1951.
7 For documentation on this and the following points, see Peter Temin and Geoffrey Peters, 'Cross-Subsidization in the Telephone Network,' *Willamette Law Review*, vol. 28, (Spring 1985), pp. 199–233.
8 William J. Baumol, 'Testimony,' FCC Docket No. 18128, Bell Exhibit, 18, October 15, 1971. Leland I. Johnson, *Competition and Cross Subsidization in the Telephone Industry*, Santa Monica, CA: The Rand Corporation, 1982, pp. 26, 34.
9 Gerald R. Faulhaber, 'Cross-Subsidization: Pricing in Public Enterprises,' *The American Economic Review*, vol. 65, (December 1975), pp. 966–77.
10 Peter Temin and Geoffrey Peters, 'Cross-Subsidization in the Telephone Network.'

Comments on the Papers
and on the Problem

6

Economics as an Historical Science

DONALD N. McCLOSKEY

Like an Iowan relative to a Californian and a New Englander, an economic historian is a convex combination of two coasts. One may note, however, that convex combinations are often superior to their end points. Still the papers by Temin and David are, I think, *exemplary* in both senses of that word, exhibiting, as they do, the economist's grasp of theory and the historian's grasp of fact. Here my critique of them will rest. We economic historians have an agreement like the one among the other hybrid economists, the mathematical theorists, discouraging critical comment about colleagues. It yields good results in power and salaries. I would not wish to be the first in the amiable history of historical economics to violate the agreement.

I have no such agreement of mutual nonaggression with the theorists. Unluckily, however, I endorse most of the answers that Kenneth Arrow gave in his paper and all that Robert Solow gave in his. I am driven to attacking the question they were asked.

This hardly seems fair, since it was not Arrow and Solow but the organizers who asked the question. What, asked the elders of the American Economic Association, is the proper relationship between economics and economic history? Or, to put it another way, is economic history necessary for an economist? Our panel of theorists answered the question correctly. Yes, said Arrow, economic history supplies data for the theories of economists, and puts the theories through toughening exercises. Yes, said Solow, a properly modest economic theory and a properly ambitious economic history could, with mutual advantage, exchange the equilibrium conditions of the one for the side conditions of the other. Arrow and Solow differ in mood. Arrow is optimistic about the present course of economic science, Solow is not. Yet both emphasize the gains from trade between economics and economic history.

In other words, Arrow and Solow accept the implicit premise that the two fields differ. That is the mistake that makes the question wrong. I say they do not differ. Since economics and economic history have the same tastes and technology and endowments they have no basis for trade. Economically speaking they are the same country.

Historical economists for their part sometimes mistake the sameness, arguing that economic history is a proper subset of economics. *Au contraire*, as they say in France. The point is that economics, in view of what it is rather than what it claims to be, is a proper subset of history.

By this I mean that economists are trying to do the same thing as historians, namely, to tell plausible stories about the past. The alternative view, which Arrow believes, is that economists are social physicists, looking for a unified field theory of society. Most economists cling to a quaint positivism supporting this notion, supposing that social physicists should predict and social engineers control. Economists are to test the theory at Iowa by its observable predictions, like the big boys at the Fermi Lab; then they are to use the theory at Harvard to design policy bombs, like the big boys at Livermore; then they are to drop them in Washington, like the big boys at Los Alamos. By emulating them the economists believe they will share in the peculiar prestige of the big (though young) physicists.

The notion is that there is a one-to-one correspondence between big physics and big economics. The econometric tests of cross-equation restrictions (*any* cross-equation restrictions, as Solow might say: don't worry, you'll find some) are supposed to correspond to crucial experiments in physics. The axiomatization of general equilibrium theory is supposed to correspond to physical theory. Since the 1940s, from Samuelson to Sargent, economists have been telling one another repeatedly that economics corresponds to some piece of physics, pure or applied, to thermodynamics or to electrical engineering. Not knowing much about how research actually proceeds in physics or engineering the audience has believed the tale. Or at any rate they have believed it enough to teach it to their students and to get themselves into the National Academy of Sciences. But they have not believed it enough to actually do it. Economists are not hunters of laws; they are hunters of stories.

The case is easiest to make with applied economics, nine-tenths of the intellectual world of economists. Like economic historians studying the history of AT&T's divestiture or of QWERTY's persistence, economists studying the activities of the CAB in 1984 try to tell a story with a beginning, a middle, and (happily in this case) an end. They succeed or fail by narrative standards. They want to connect one event to another. For all their talk of hypothesis testing they are not actually testing, say, some theory of regulation (no wonder: the 'theory' amounts to saying that people usually do what is advisable).

Telling stories is how we make sense of what has happened. Stories tell: 'Where does all this stuff come from?' Once upon a time there was a big bang . . . 'How did we get so rich?' There were once some tinkerers in Britain . . . 'How did the French Revolution spread to Europe?' There was once in Corsica a son of Carlo and Letizia Bonaparte . . . 'What is our life?' There was once in Bethlehem . . .[1] The attempt by Carl Hempel and others in the 1940s to force the storytelling into a positivist model has failed (even Hempel knew that historians write stories, not laws). It works no better in the branch of economic history known as applied economics.

Applied economics commonly tells its stories these days with statistics and mathematics rather than mere words. But the figures of speech it uses are beside the point. Simulation of the American economy in recession or of the Midwest in the railroad age are no less stories than *Through the Looking Glass*, with which indeed they share other features:

> 'I can't believe *that*!' said Alice.
> 'Can't you?' the Queen said in a pitying tone . . . 'I daresay you haven't had much practice . . . When I was your age, I always did it for half-an-hour a day. Why, sometimes I've believed as many as six impossible things before breakfast!'

The belief comes from mathematical storytelling. The rhetoric of statistics misleads the econometrician into thinking that by running a hyperplane through his beliefs about the statistics he is subjecting his beliefs to 'test.' But he is not testing them – as he can understand by recognizing how insignificant are his tests of significance – but expressing them, telling them, fitting them to the crude facts, in a word, simulating them. Simulation, the engineer's word for the telling of hypothetical stories disciplined by fact, is the economist's main figure of speech.

Historians do it, too. The historian of medieval English law wishes to tell a story that by 1300 someone recently dispossessed of his property (a victim of 'novel disseisin') could take it back only with the help of the king and not by vigilante justice. He imagined how Bracton could have come to his four-day rule of ejectment or how purchasers of land would have needed protection against the death of their seller.[2] Like an engineer or applied economist, he practices the trick of simulating the important possibilities, disciplined by expert knowledge of the social structure. The economic historian of medieval open fields imagines how scattered plots would affect risk and simulates the result mathematically. Both historians simulate in aid of a story. So does the economist trying to fit his equation for the demand for money: they all want to tell stories, of how the king won the rule of law, how communal agriculture rose and decayed, how the Federal Reserve has done its job since the War.

If applied economists were law-hunting instead of storytelling they would predict. As the Queen said, 'It's a poor sort of memory that only works backwards.' The pressures to try to work the memory forward are immense. The businesspeople, the bureaucrats, the journalists, his mother – all want the economist to tell what the future will bring. The governing metaphor is weather forecasting.

However, it is becoming pretty clear that economists are poor predictors. On practical and, what is more depressing, theoretical grounds the economists cannot forecast well. The cold fronts are listening, and the forecasters are themselves part of the weather.

If economists go on indulging the misapprehensions of their customers, issuing predictions about next month's exchange rate or next spring's interest rate, the loss of reputation when the customers catch on will be large, and richly deserved. It would be better to declare a victory and go home. The failure to forecast *is* a victory for the science. Precisely because economic science is such a fine way of telling stories about the past there are no unexploited opportunities lying about to be seized by professors in battered tweed jackets. A leading principle of economics, after all, is the American question: If you're so smart, why aren't you rich?

Applied economics, then, is the economic history of the recent past. When done well it has the air of good history written by someone who has taken Differential Equations 152. But the hard case is supposed to be economic theory itself, and its handmaiden, econometrics. Surely these are 'nomothetic': 'law giving.' Surely this is the physics, as Arrow claims, the laws for all time (or at least until the next regime, or until once again the stationarity breaks down). In such an analogy, as Arrow says, economic history would be the geology to the physics of economic theory, applying the laws developed in the lab to tell a story in the field.

Solow argues that this characterization of economic theory is unpersuasive, and I agree. To his weighty case I can only add a further question. What *are* these laws of the social physics? When economists name something a Law, in the style of Boyle's Law or Ohm's Law, there is commonly a playful irony involved, a sense that after all it is a poor thing, a mere fact, such as Denison's Law or Okun's Law (whose recent histories have not been happy).

The permanent laws that economists believe are bold enough. The Law of Demand or the Law of Profitable Entry, for instance, irritate anthropologists and have other features commending them for use. But the scientific ceremonies of testing have little to to with their persuasiveness. How many economists, for instance, have been persuaded of the Law of Demand by the ceremonies involving complete systems of demand equations popular amongst the Netherlanders? Really and truly? Or again, are economists really going to succeed in 'testing' the law of rational expectations? And if they do, will the test be worth anything beyond the telling of a good story about 1933 or 1984? What *are* those 'results' so long promised by econometrics?

Understand, I (like Solow) am no machine breaker. Theory is thinking about economic behavior, and econometrics is thinking about economic statistics. We're all in favor of thinking. The gains in penetration of understanding forced on economists by 200 years of economic thinking, and in breadth of understanding forced by 100 years of economic history, have been immense. But the gains in lucidity forced on economists by the 40 years of mathematization of economic theory and statistics have been large, too. It is the false analogy with physics to which Solow and I are objecting, not to the use of the calculus of variations when the dog is, after all, purusing his master. It is not the formal techniques of physics themselves that are the problem but the metaphysical incantations that come along with them.

To put it another way, if economists need a big brother to admire, it should probably not be the physicist. Economists are more like geologists or paleontologists, telling stories of the

Pacific plate or the panda's thumb. There is no prediction, no experiment. There is just mucking about in libraries and computing centers, thinking the stories through and checking to see if they square with historical facts laid up in archives. If economists need a big brother, he could come from these historical sciences, or from history itself. A field that took the English legal historian Frederick Maitland or the French rural historian Marc Bloch for its heroes would not do badly.

Except, of course, in pay. A corrupting feature of the myth of social physics is its claim to undergird an insightful, profitable, purchasable social engineering. But of course if economics were to give up the nomothetic myth it would have to give up, too, the 'big con of big science,' namely, that the study of the age of the universe or the character of quarks, like the seventeenth model of a possible world of international finance, is more *useful* than the study of Indo–European vowels or the structure of Latin poetry. This, however, is another matter, this relationship between an economics that saw itself plain and the other half of our civilization.

Anyhow, the cat is out of the bag, the shoe is on the other foot, the emperor is without his clothes. Economics is neither social physics nor social engineering: it is more like a peculiar variant of social history. Economics does not merely have a lot to learn from history: history is what it is.

Notes

1   Wayne C. Booth, *Modern Dogma and the Rhetoric of Assent*, Chicago University of Chicago Press, 1974, p. 186.
2   Donald W. Sutherland, *The Assize of Novel Disseisin*, Oxford: Oxford University Press, 1973, pp. 103, 113.

7

Professor Arrow on Economic Analysis and Economic History

W. W. ROSTOW

Professor Arrow's thoughtful paper[1] came to rest, as I read it, on the incapacity of modern economic analysis to deal with the full range of variables at work in economic history and on the potentialities for mutual reinforcement by the two disciplines. This note is designed to sharpen the proposition and to draw certain implications for a more appropriate relation of economic theory both to economic history and to problems in the contemporary world economy. Obviously, Professor Arrow is in no way bound by the conclusions drawn here.

Like Professor Arrow, I regret the ignorance of history among most contemporary economists and, even more, among the current products of our major graduate schools of economics. But the problem is more serious than that. The economic theory our students are taught is often so structured that it is capable of dealing satisfactorily with only a narrow range of problems, either historical or contemporary. There is a great deal to be said for the use of mathematical and econometric method if it is treated strictly as one among other tools to illuminate or to solve serious problems. There is nothing to be said for the tendency to regard the mastery of these techniques as an objective in itself or to cut problems down to a size that permits their management with the limited capabilities which currently fashionable methods provide.

Professor Rostow's comment was not made at the meeting of the American Economic Association in Dallas (December, 1984), but was submitted subsequently.

This is the root of the problem of relating economic theory to the flow of events in the active world, past or present. Faculty club conversation would, no doubt, be more civilized among economists if they knew more history. But if we are to bring economic analysis and economic history into the regular and fruitful mutual support implied by Professor Arrow's argument, we must try to solve in our time what might be called the Malthus–Ricardo problem.

Working in close communication from 1811 to Ricardo's death in 1823 – with evident mutual respect, friendship, and a rare capacity to place the pursuit of truth above their clashing theoretical formulations – they could never resolve their differences.

Each tried to explain the impasse.

Malthus suggested that the difference arose between those who made a 'precipitate attempt to simplify and generalize' and 'their more practical opponents [who] draw too hasty inferences from a frequent appeal to partial facts . . .'[2] Malthus concluded: 'In political economy the desire to simplify has occasioned an unwillingness to acknowledge the operation of more causes than one in the production of particular effects . . . The first business of philosophy is to account for things as they are . . . where unforeseen causes may possibly be in operation . . . an accurate yet comprehensive attention to facts is necessary.'

Ricardo isolated 'one great cause of our difference in opinion' in somewhat different but quite consistent terms: Malthus's concern with 'immediate and temporary effects' as opposed to his effort to fix his 'whole attention on the permanent state of things which will result from them.' Ricardo concluded: 'Perhaps you estimate these temporary effects too highly, whilst I am too much disposed to undervalue them.'[3]

The counterpoint runs on to our own times. Take D. H. Robertson in Malthus's mood:[4]

We must wait with respectful patience while the econometricians decide whether their elaborate methods are really capable of covering such models with flesh and blood. But I confess that to me at least the forces at work seem so complex, the question whether even the few selected parameters can be relied on to stay put through the cycle or between cycles so doubtful, that I wonder whether more truth will not in the end be wrung from interpretive studies of the crude data of the general type contained in this volume [*A Study of Industrial Fluctuation*], but more intensive, more scrupulously-worded and more expert.

And, Milton Friedman in the spirit of Ricardo:[5] 'A hypothesis is important if it "explains" much by little, that is, if it abstracts the common and crucial elements from the mass of complex and detailed circumstances surrounding the phenomena to be explained and permits valid predictions on the basis of them alone.' The problem is, of course, that both Ricardo's and Friedman's simple, powerful hypotheses, standing alone, failed to yield valid predictions.

If we are to make progress with the Malthus–Ricardo problem rather than fruitlessly to harangue each other or even recapture the gracious spirit in which these two great predecessors tried to define the chasm between them, there are different tasks to be undertaken by both the theorist and the historian.

The theorist must be prepared to try to do three things. First, he must acknowledge the profound limitations of present sophisticated mathematical and econometric methods as ways of coming to grips with the active world. Second, he must try to render dynamic in formal theory some of the variables now fixed 'for purposes of reasoning' or on grounds of 'analytic tractability.'[6] Third, he must accept as part of the theorist's fundamental mission that he budget time and energy to acquire 'an accurate yet comprehensive' knowledge of the factors. It is not enough for the theorist to take the view that he is prepared to be helpful if only the historian would organise the data in usable form, with all the parameters properly estimated.[7] This stricture implies that the end product is likely to be a good deal less elegant than he would like. The compensation is that he has come closer to accounting 'for things as they are' – or were.

The economic historian, too, has some things to do which he is generally not doing. First, he must refuse to accept current mainstream neo-classical economics as a sufficient theoretical framework for his work. It has sufficed for important studies on certain limited problems; e.g. the diffusion of the reaper (cited by Professor Arrow), tariffs and the emergence of the modern American iron industry, the sources of expansion of American cotton textile production before the Civil War. In my view, it was an insufficient framework for the study of the railroads or slavery and would prove grossly inadequate if the cliometricians were to face up, as they should, to a systematic history of the growth and fluctuations of the American economy over the past two centuries. Second, having abandoned his subservience to received theory, the historian must play a more active role in helping the theorist elaborate and dynamize his models to render them more relevant to great problems in economic history. Finally, the historian, working with the theorist, must strain to develop from the data the best approximations for all the relevant variables he and the theorist agree must be taken into account.

Now, how, as a practical matter, can such intense working partnerships between the theorist and the collector and analyst of evidence be brought about? I doubt that methodological exhortation, or even formal concord, can do the trick. What is needed, I believe, is a shared, strong – even passionate – interest in important, relevant contemporary problems. Professor Arrow referred to the vitality formerly exhibited by business cycle history. That vitality came from a determination to understand the business cycle and to alleviate its grave human and social costs. This aspiration led Wesley C. Mitchell, D. H. Robertson, A. C. Pigou, and some of us in the next generation to concern ourselves with the history as well as the theory of business cycles. After the Second World War the problems of growth in the developing regions played a similar catalytic role for the theory and history, and generated linkages between the two domains. Around us and ahead, there are many unsolved problems with an historical dimension, where concerted effort might be fruitful, linking theorists to historians and other scholars who are prepared to pay 'comprehensive attention to facts.' Here are a few examples:

Technology and Employment: By what mechanisms did major new technologies introduced over the past two centuries, up to and including the present, generate both additional employment and additional unemployment? In the contemporary world this kind of analysis will require breaking out of the tyranny of the Standard Industrial Classifications and working from input–output employment matrices modified for these purposes, taking account *inter alia* of service employment generated by the new technologies.

Increasing and Diminishing Returns: How, over two centuries, was the tendency to diminishing returns held at bay; and what are the prospects for the next 50–75 years when global population moves to a probable peak? In theory, this requires, as Marshall clearly perceived, a facing up to the embarrassment to equilibrium economics presented by the existence of increasing returns.

The Rich Country, Poor Country Problem: The problem confronted by a relatively rich country which stirs by its example an imitative 'fermentation' in a poor country was first lucidly formulated and prescribed for by David Hume.[8] It moved off the center of the stage in economic theory with the British take-off of the 1780s. Two centuries later it is back with a vengeance as the US contemplates Japan, Japan contemplates South Korea, Taiwan, and the dynamism of other developing countries in the Pacific Basin and, in time, China and India. How a front runner maintains (or fails to maintain) his place in the inescapable race is, evidently, a central problem for the future of US society, as the state of our balance of payments suggests.

In all these problems – and a good many others any one of us could cite – the relevance of history is authentic; modern economic theory and econometrics are usable but insufficient; and concerted effort to study the problem as a whole is likely to generate both new and significant theoretical propositions and the mobilization of hitherto underutilized historical and other empirical evidence.

There are, of course, theorists and historians who will not be interested in this kind of intensive sustained collaboration centered on the search for solutions to urgent, practical problems. There are even likely to be some in both theory and economic history who regard explicit attention to problems of current policy as beneath the dignity of their disciplines. Debate with those who cherish such notions is not only fruitless, but counter-productive. Our disciplines do and should contain men and women of different interests and tastes. But the brute fact is that both economic theory and economic history have evolved over the past two centuries in response to specific and identifiable problems in the active world. And that is the route we will have to follow if the current process of diminishing returns in both disciplines is to be reversed.

That is, of course, not the only way to look at the matter. Robert Solow once remarked, towards the close of a conference in 1960 embracing both theorists and economic historians:[9] '. . . perhaps the best thing might be for economic historians and model builders to remain friends, but no more – for the economists to misuse historians' data and for the historians to misunderstand the economists' theories.' But a quarter century later the results of an attenuating friendship beween the two disciplines cannot be regarded on either side with satisfaction or complacency. I take it Professor Arrow called on us to do better. I agree.

Notes

1 Kenneth J. Arrow, 'Economic History: A Necessary Though Not Sufficient Condition for an Economist. Maine and Texas', *AEA Papers and Proceedings*, vol. 75, no. 2 (May 1985), pp. 320–3.

2 T. R. Malthus, *Principles of Political Economy*, New York: Kelley, reprinted August 1951, extracted from pp. 4–12.

3 Piero Sraffa and M. H. Dobb (eds.), *The Works and Correspondence of David Ricardo*, vol. VII, *Letters 1816–1818*, Cambridge: Cambridge University Press, for the Royal Economic Society, 1952, p. 120.

4 D. H. Robertson, *A Study of Industrial Fluctuation* (1915), reprinted by the London School of Economics and Political Science, No. 8 in Series of Reprints of Scarce Works on Political Economy, 1948, p. xvii.

5 Milton Friedman, 'The Methodology of Positive Economics,' in *Essays in Positive Economics*, Chicago: University of Chicago Press, 1953, p. 14.

6 The full context of the two phrases is as follows: 'The classical theory [of international trade] assumes as fixed for purposes of reasoning, the very things which . . . should be the chief objective of study' (John Williams, 'The Theory of International Trade Reconsidered,' *Economic Journal*, vol. 39, no. 154 (June 1929), p. 196). 'It should be quite obvious to any careful reader of this book that our analysis so far is based on a very large number of assumptions, some of which can be justified only on the grounds of their analytic tractability . . . further work may require some radical reconsideration of the premises underlying the present type of inquiry' (Sukhamoy Chakravarty, *Capital and Development Planning*, Cambridge, MA: M.I.T. Press, 1969, p. 246).

7 See, for example, Robert Solow in W. W. Solow (ed.), *The Economics of Take-off into Sustained Economic Growth*, London: Macmillan, 1963, pp. 471–2.

8 Istvan Hont, 'The Rich Country–Poor Country Debate in Scottish Classical Political Economy,' in Istvan Hont and Michael Ignatieff (eds.), *Wealth and Virtue: The Shaping of Political Economy in the Scottish Enlightenment*, ch. 11, Cambridge: Cambridge University Press, 1983, pp. 271–315.

9 Robert Solow in W. W. Rostow (ed.) *The Economics of Take-off*, 1963, p. 474.

8

History and the Future of Economics

GAVIN WRIGHT

The papers by Arrow, Davis, Solow and Temin all reach the same conclusion, that knowledge of and appreciation for history is important for economics and ought to be an integral part of the discipline. They arrive at this point by quite different routes, David and Temin by illustrative examples, Arrow by analogies to other disciplines, and Solow by critique of the conception of economics as an axiomatically-based hard science. All the arguments are reasonable and persuasive, so it might seem that there is no further need for discussion. However, I want to be a bit troublesome just the same, though I have no plans to reach any different conclusion. What I want to question is the idea that economics and history can hope to have a congenial, complementary relationship, like physics and geology. Economic theory formulates general principles, while history studies particular events. These events may illustrate the general laws in part, but they will also reflect particular historical conditions and circumstances. Hence, the need for historical specialists who are also trained in economics. It sounds like a happy marriage, but in practice there are deeper differences which are not easily reconcilable.

One place to begin is with the issue posed by Arrow, whether and in what sense the laws of economics are 'historically conditioned.' Arrow cites John Stuart Mill as an example of a theorist who made it clear that the classical laws of value 'held only in an economy in which the exchange was governed by markets.' At first blush it sounds broad-minded and flexible for a theorist to acknowledge that his intellectual edifice may not be as universally rigorous as its formal structure might imply. But the same statements may be read less favorably as a cop-out. In his most explicit statement, Mill certainly did acknowledge that 'competition . . . has only become in any considerable degree the governing principle of contracts, at a comparatively modern period.' He thought that rents were mainly determined until recent time by *custom*, which was still a powerful force in many areas. Even prices, he thought, were subject to custom, in retail trade (for example), 'modified from time to time by notions existing in the minds of purchasers and sellers of some kind of equity or justice.' But what significance do these vestiges of the past have for Mill's economic theory? He writes:

> These observations must be received as a general correction to be applied whenever relevant, whether expressly mentioned or not, to the conclusions contained in the subsequent portions of this treatise. Our reasonings must, in general, proceed as if the known and natural effects of competition were actually produced by it, in all cases where it is not restrained by some positive obstacle. Where competition, though free to exist, does not exist, or where it exists, but has its natural consequences overruled by any other agency, the conclusions will fail more or less of being applicable. (*Principles*, Book II, ch. 4, p. 247)

In other words, these theories hold except when they don't! But I do not call it a cop-out because he acknowledges exceptions and lags. I call it a cop-out as far as history is concerned, because, though he presents *implicitly* a clear and powerful view of history, this view does not inform the analysis itself. History has no integral role, but it is only a 'general correction to be applied whenever relevant.'

Though Mill himself was of course a man of broad learning in history and many other subjects, his conception of the relationship between history and economics was primitive. Yet it is one which still widely prevails. 'History' is seen as a remote

78

time of 'traditional' or 'customary' behavior, at any rate so far removed from modern practices and thinking that it is not directly relevant. But in what specific way is a theory institutionally or historically specific? Usually it is not clear; in fact theorists strive for the greatest generality possible as a matter of principle. Saying that 'exchange must be governed by markets' is not specific enough. What is a market? Economists well understand, and it is one of the first things we teach, that 'markets' and 'market forces' may be present even without an explicit, visible, organized market place. Economists can find them anywhere in history as well as in contemporary life. But it is an empty triumph to show that economic theory is flexible enough to account for virtually any human experience in any epoch, because theory is then exposed as so universal as to be vacuous.

The problem as I see it is that useful economic theories *are* historically conditioned, but economists do not often think hard about exactly what these conditions are, and they do not welcome pressure in this direction. This is why history and economics will not be a comfortable bedfellows. But it is all the *more* reason why economic history taught by instructors trained in economics should be part of every graduate program.

Let me give another example from a completely different branch of economics. Most readers of Keynes' *General Theory* have taken it to be a model suited to a mature capitalist economy. That seems to be implicit in the conception of labor markets, for example, and we know that it was the persistent unemployment in interwar Britain followed by the Great Depression in the 1930s that Keynes was trying to interpret. At many points he stressed that full employment problems would be more severe for a wealthy nation than for a poor one. But if we ask exactly what institutional features of such a mature economy cause it to function as it does, we find that Keynes does not tell us. Not through carelessness but through an active effort to avoid anything that tied the analysis to particular institutional structures: it purported to be a 'general theory.' In fact, Keynes himself could not resist the temptation to go back and resuscitate mercantilist doctrines from as far back as the sixteenth century, even applying his formulation at one point to ancient Egypt. This failure to locate his theoretical mechanisms in historical time reflects the deep-set orientation of economists toward the discipline, and has certainly stayed with us since then.

This tradition of *not quite saying* what the historical context is, in my opinion, actively diminishes the quality of economic debate in this country. Macro-economics, for example, is divided into all-encompassing schools of thought like 'monetarism' or 'Keynesianism' each of which tries to interpret the whole of history in terms of its philosophy. This search for the 'one true model' almost proscribes serious investigation of how the macro-economy has changed, as it certainly has, from the 1910s to the 1920s, from the 1930s and 1950s to the 1970s and 1980s. What we should be asking is what it was about the economy that made the simple Keynesian model seem so appropriate for the 1930s through the 1950s. But despite all of the assaults on Keynesian economics, this question has certainly not been at the center of the research agenda for macro-economics. Economic historians should have been bolder and noisier. They should have made more trouble for the theorists than they actually did. They should have been more insistent on keeping the historical perspective always in view.

The lack of historical perspective in economics is not just a matter of refinement and breadth; it is a real handicap to the students we teach, from a very practical standpoint. If we were to ask just what the purpose of economic instruction is, why we teach it and why students study it, surely one major class of reasons involves the hope that the operation and performance of the American economy will be better if policies are developed by or with the advice of people with training in economics. We hope undergraduate students will be better-informed lawyers, politicians, businessmen and voters; graduate students will actually conduct studies and offer advice. If this is so, if the whole operation has something to do with improving the performance of the US economy, then it is perfectly scandalous that the majority of economics students complete their studies with no knowledge whatsoever about how the United States became the leading economy in the world, as of the first half of the twentieth century. What sort of doctor would diagnose and prescribe without taking a medical history? In trying to choose a textbook for an introductory course, I have recently examined a large number of texts, and can report that they say virtually nothing on this subject, nor do they convey to American students that American economic pre-eminence is in any way remarkable or puzzling or in need of explanation. If they do discuss long-term growth and contemporary problems, they treat the past in much the way that John Stuart Mill did, in a sense. He assumed that the past was dominated by simple custom, an uncomplicated and presumably unchanging world where things were at least clear. That is more or less the way our textbooks, and perhaps most American economists, think about the American past: that economic growth just happened, year by year, in an inexorable self-sustained way as far back as anyone really cares to go. This conception of history is, of course, not the same as Mill's but the two have in common the treatment of the past as an undifferentiated lump with a fairly simple economic structure.

However, if it is instead the case that some peculiar and historically specific factors were at work in the rise of the American economy to world prominence over the century from 1850 to 1950, then the impression conveyed by the texts is not merely oversimplified, but seriously wrong and potentially mischievous. Even posing the simple question: why was the US the richest country in the world in 1950? and spending some hard lecture and study time on it, forces thought in constructive directions. It is not that there is an easy answer out there waiting to be uncovered. But you don't get far into the subject without seeing the importance of historical circumstances, and this inevitably leads one to ask how these circumstances may have changed in more recent years. Any thoughtful answer will have a distinct effect on one's thinking about policies and performance in the US economy since 1950. This is the difference between economic history and geology. Geological time is too long and slow to produce change within our lifetimes. It is effectively over, for practical purposes. But in economic life we are actually living in historical time, if not every day and year, then decade by decade. Within living memory national economies have gone from insignificance to world prominence, from robust health to stagnation and vice versa. We have seen the rise and decline of whole systems of world trade and payments, as well as the rise and decline of entire systems of economic thought and understanding. It is rarely safe to predict the future, but it does not seem risky to expect that such periodic revolutionary mutations will continue to occur. And these are the stuff of economic history. It is imprudent and unfair to send economists out into the world without even a rudimentary education in the subject.

9

A Further Comment

CHARLES P. KINDLEBERGER

The session devoted to economic history at the annual meeting of the American Economic Association at Dallas in December 1984, organized by William N. Parker and chaired by W. Arthur Lewis, offered papers by Arrow, Temin, Solow and David, followed by discussion from McCloskey and Wright. It was one of the most enthusiastically received sessions on the program, both at the time of the meeting and subsequently when the papers, though not the discussion, appeared in the *Papers and Proceedings* issue of the *American Economic Review* in May 1985. As arranger of the program of the Dallas meetings, I have received evidence of this from many sources, by word of mouth and by letter. It was not entirely clear, perhaps, whether the enthusiasm had its origin in the wit and verve of the panel and discussants, in the accessibility of the several messages, as compared with high theory and low description, or in genuine agreement with the methodological point that economics may have strayed from its true path in its emphasis on mathematical theory and formal econometric testing, away from its roots in the real world, viz. in the experience of real economies in the past.

An arranger of programs at AEA conventions is allowed wide latitude, up to a point, to shape the program to conform to his or her own interests. Beyond that point, the interests of the profession at large take over, with tremendous pressure applied by one and all to find outlet for the flood of economic research in progress. The session on economic history belonged to the first category, and was to an extent an *apologia pro vita mea*, rooted also in my concern that economic history is losing its place in economic curricula. At MIT, for example, one term of economic history has been a requirement for the doctorate for at least 35 years. In recent years, students have had the option of American History with Peter Temin, Russian with Evsey Domar, or European with me. Since Domar and I retired, no economist with history as a string to his or her bow has been hired. The difficulty in hiring an economic historian today, as compared with a generation ago, is that the department's standards in theory and econometrics are so elevated that someone who would seem to economic historians to be deeply versed in history will have had little time or perhaps even commitment to attain to the level of theory demanded of present-day colleagues. When Temin is on leave, moreover, or should his interests diverge from the classic bill of fare in American history, there is no effective way to meet the present requirement, unless by a potpourri of the scraps of historical knowledge of other members of the department. This expedient has been tried at Harvard in years when economic historians in the department were unavailable to teach the standard courses in economic history. Students found the staccato shifts among bite-size nuggets of European, American, Russian, Chinese annd Latin American economic history disconcerting. When the experiment was repeated the following year, they flocked in droves to MIT for normal fare under our exchange arrangement. With fewer and fewer economists and historians interested in teaching economic history, the requirement appears to be doomed. The question arises whether this is the direction in which economics ought to go.

Septuagenarians (or octogenarians, depending upon how you start counting) always think the world is changing for the worse. In my case, additionally, 12 years away from the academy before, during and after the Second World War meant that my professional formation lacked a solid foundation of mathematical economics and econometrics along which I could develop my interest in international economics. In a sour-grapes mood, I have lately suggested that much of the field today is bankrupt.[1] It may be pure rationalization but nevertheless I feel that my late-blooming interest in economic history derives only partly from an inability to swim with the current fashionable tide. I think it has some basis in a conviction that at the educational margin today, economic history, or perhaps more accurately, historical economics, provides a deeper understanding of the way the world works than more theory and more manipulation of numbers.

Let me illustrate from the field of tariffs – a standard subject of both international economics and economic history. As a textbook writer, I have been reasonably competent in tariff theory as it derives from the pure theory of trade, the Heckscher–Ohlin–Samuelson model, the Stolper–Samuelson theorem, factor–price equalization, Meade on trade and welfare, theories of public choice, the theory of the second-best, and the like. If, however, one asks how much do they explain of tariff history, singly or en masse, or how much do they assist an economist to forecast what will happen in the next decades in world trade, the answer must be 'not a great deal.' This realization first dawned on me when I was studying the response of various European countries to the fall in the price of wheat after 1880. By that date, the cost of carrying wheat from the great plains of the world in North and South America, in Australia and in the Ukraine to Europe had fallen sharply, raising the price of wheat for the producer and lowering it to the consumer. (Most trade theory, incidentally, assumes an absence of transport costs.) The cost of ocean shipping had fallen with the coming of the iron-clad, propeller-driven steamship, while the railroad had reduced the cost of carrying the grain from the producing plains to the ports of shipment. Simple trade theory would have predicted that European countries would either liquidate agriculture or impose tariffs: the choice to be decided presumably by calling on the theory of public choice and depending largely on whether the abundant or the scarce factor was politically dominant. Of the five countries studied, the theory predicted well in only two: Britain where the capital-intensive manufacturing sector was abundant, and after the Reform Bill of 1832, politically dominant, and Germany where the dominant interest was the grain-growing Junkers, and protection was applied. French, Italian and Danish responses involved variations. For sociological and political reasons, France sought protection for the family farm, found in all 90 departments of the country. The Italian government delayed imposing a tariff, and while the decision to act was being taken, Italians emigrated in large numbers to the Americas, in shocking violation of the assumptions of trade theory that factors are immobile between countries. The Danish reaction was perhaps the most interesting: the country transformed itself to a grain-importing country, shifting its comparative advantage dynamically from grain to meat and dairy products that relied on imported feed inputs. The transformation was aided by the strong British demand for a hearty breakfast, and made possible by two crucial innovations, one mechanical, the other social: the cream separator and the producer cooperative that permitted the combination of small-scale output and large-scale marketing.[2]

Subsequent research on the rise of free trade in Europe and on the foreign economic policy of the United States uncovered still further considerations not alluded to in economic theory. Political reasons were involved when Napoleon III agreed to the Cobden–Chevalier treaty of 1860 in order to gain British neutrality for French military adventures in Italy; Bismarck too took up a low-tariff policy prior to 1875, when highly protectionist Austria challenged Prussia for leadership in the *Zollverein*.[3] In the United States both North and South, a curious cultural lag persisted far into the twentieth century. In the North, Senator Robert Taft clung to the traditional Republican high tariff policy in the 1940s when his home town in his native state, Cincinnati, Ohio, was exporting machine tools worldwide; in the South, Senator Walter George remained a staunch free trader long after the production of cotton, an export crop, had moved west to Texas and California, and cotton textiles that relied on tariffs, had moved to Georgia from New England. Another example showing the limitations of even the subtleties of classical theory for prediction is Stephen Magee's demonstration[4] that pressure groups testifying for and against tariffs in the American Congress are organized by industry – as noted long ago by Cairnes – and not by factors of production. Labor and capital are found on each side of the argument for and against protection, not massed, one against the other.

I go on at too great length perhaps about trade and tariffs, but the relevance of economic history to today's pressing concerns in both economic theory and economic policy can be illustrated in other fields – economic growth, international capital flows and debt, fluctuations and financial stability, and at a more profound social level the deep depressions in the last quarter of the nineteenth century and the 1930s. Perhaps the sharpest clash between theory and history is over the question of rationality. Rationality is the axiom on which theory is built, but the logical postulate is far from ensuring that all markets always behave in rational fashion. The record is strewn with instances of the fallacy of composition – each participant rational, though with differences in intelligence and information, but the totality acting dysfunctionally, as in the example of theatre-goers escaping from a fire, of euphoria that overshoots, of limited horizons.

To express a need for economic history to test the generality of economic models is not to argue against models[5]. On the contrary, both the economist and the economic historians need models to isolate the basic forces at work in a given process, and remove as much noise as possible. Bagehot put it in a sentence emphasized by Alfred Marshall in the latter's introduction to Bagehot's *Economic Studies*: 'If you attempt to solve such problems [complex problems of commerce] without some apparatus of method, you are as sure to fail as if you try to take a modern fortress – a Metz or Belfort – by common assault: you must have guns to attack the one, and method to attack the other.'[6]

I would argue, however, that, like economic history, models are not sufficient. One day at the luncheon table at the MIT Faculty Club a few years ago, a young colleague in my presence asked an older one to help him find a use for an interesting model he had just developed. When I quote this among economists I generally draw a nervous laugh. I find a bit faddish the modern practice of a literary economist asking a technical colleague to produce a mathematical appendix for an analysis that is already clear and logical. I would agree, to be sure, that economic intuition cannot be relied on alone, although it is also necessary. In the same passage as that above, Bagehot quotes Coleridge who said to a 'sensible lady,' 'Madam, I accept your conclusion, but you must let me find the logic for it.'[7] I would argue, further, that economic intuition that constitutes an essential ingredient in analysis is developed better by wider knowledge of economic history than by the present fashion of pursuing mathematics to deeper and deeper degrees of sophistication.

Economic theory, states Schumpeter,[8] quoting Joan Robinson with approval, is a box of tools. James Meade has observed that economics is well equipped with tools, and that the problem is to find the right combination.[9] It seems to me to be a weakness of economics – one that economic history helps overcome – that its practitioners from time to time get carried away by a single model. I happened to discuss Mancur Olson's *Rise and Decline of Nations*[10] at a seminar at which he was present, applauded the model in which 'distributive coalitions' blocked legislative agenda, produced stalemate and slowed down economic growth, but observed that he claimed too much for it. His response was disarmingly frank: 'To the boy with a new hammer, the whole world looks like a nail.' The same is true of economists with old models. In balance-of-payments analysis, economists tend to belong to one of three schools, emphasizing price (the elasticities school of Machlup), spending (the 'absorption' Keynesian model of Sidney Alexander), or money (Mundell). In the long run, the three theories converge, since markets for goods, income and money all have to clear in equilibrium. In the short run, however, it is a mistake to lean exclusively on a single model, one or another can take the lead – although in my judgment the notion that economies vary exports and imports in order to equate money demand to money supply is counter-intuitive and thus most unlikely. To embrace only one is to succumb to the appeal of explanations exhibiting simply analytical elegance, parsimony and 'power'. Similar reasons argue against forcing the economist to choose sides in the debates between Keynesianism versus monetarism, the banking school versus the currency school, the balance-of-payments explanation of the German inflation of 1923 as against the quantity theory, stock versus flow approaches to the theory of international capital movements, and many more hotly debated issues. The fallacy of the undistributed middle warns against forced choices among theories that are sometimes substitutes, sometimes complements, sometimes applicable *seriatim* in one order or another.

In a recent review of two books on development, Jan Tinbergen[11] insists that there is only one approach to economic analysis:

1 List the variables involved in the problem (this is as far, he asserts, as literary economists get);
2 formulate the relationships assumed to exist among the variables;
3 collect empirical data;
4 test the assumed relationships until statistically reliable results are obtained;
5 use the model with the estimated parameters to obtain optimal policy.

The message of the symposium revealed especially by the 'stories' of Temin and David, and the 'conversations' of Solow and McCloskey, is that this is too mechanical.

Let me return once again to Bagehot:

> Effectual political economy, political economy which in complex problems succeeds, is a very difficult thing; something altogether more abstruse and difficult, as well as more conclusive, than that which many of those who rush in upon it have a notion of. It is an abstract science which labours under a special hardship. Those who are conversant with its abstractions are usually without a true contact with its facts; those who are in contact with its facts, have usually little sympathy with and little cognizance of its abstractions.[12]

The economic historians and theorists represented in this volume are not concerned that economics will neglect the abstractions. They worry, however, whether as the subject becomes more and more technical, time will be left to allow and encourage students of economics to develop and maintain 'a true contact with its facts.'

I end with recantation. In finishing off the book *Economic Growth in France and Britain, 1851–1950*, discouraged by the plethora of competing mono-causal explanations for a general-equilibrium problem, and goaded by an agreeable editor to end the book with a bang, I wrote: 'Economic history, like all history, is absorbing, beguiling, great fun. But for scientific purposes can it be taken seriously?'[13]

This gave offense, and offense was taken. General equilibrium remains difficult to the point of being impossible, both in theory and in historical problems such as growth. But I now take economic history seriously indeed, and urge a similar born-again attitude on my fellow current and prospective economists.

Notes

1 Charles P. Kindleberger, 'Assets and Liabilities of International Economics: The Postwar Bankruptcy of Theory and Policy,' in Monte dei Paschi di Siena, *Economic Notes*, no. 2 (1982), pp. 47–64.

2 Charles P. Kindleberger, 'Group Behavior and International Trade,' *Journal of Political Economy* (1951); reprinted in *idem, Economic Response*, Cambridge, MA: Harvard University Press, 1978, pp. 19–38.

3 Charles P. Kindleberger, 'The Rise of Free Trade in Western Europe, 1820–1875,' *Journal of Economic History* (1975); reprinted in *idem, Economic Response*, Cambridge, MA: Harvard University Press, 1978, pp. 39–65.

4 Stephen P. Magee, 'Three Simple Tests of the Stolper–Samuelson Theorem,' in P. Oppenheimer (ed.), *Issues in International Economics*, London: Oriel Press, 1980, pp. 138–52.

5 Leland B. Yeager, 'The Image of the Gold Standard,' in Michael D. Bordo and Anna J. Schwartz (eds.), *A Retrospective on the Classical Gold Standard, 1821–1931*, Chicago: University of Chicago Press, 1984, pp. 651–69. Leland Yeager objects to appealing to history to discriminate between correct and incorrect economic theories, saying 'The facts underlying or informing economic theory "ought" to be more basic, dependable and enduring and more firmly rooted in human nature and the human condition than the contingent facts of specific historical conditions and episodes.' It is hard for me to see that the facts of history are more contingent than the 'facts underlying economic theory' which I can only regard as assumptions.

6 Walter Bagehot, *Economic Studies*, 1876; reprinted in Norman St. John-Stevas, *The Collected Works of Walter Bagehot*, Vol. IX *The Economist*, (London, 1978), pp. 196, 229.

7 Walter Bagehot, *Economic Studies*, 1876, p. 227.

8 Joseph A. Schumpeter, *A History of Economic Analysis*, edited from manuscript by Elizabeth Boody Schumpeter, London: Allen & Unwin, 1954, p. 15.

9 Mark Blaug, *Great Economists Since Keynes*, Brighton, Sussex: Wheatsheaf Books, 1985, p. 163.

10 Mancur Olson, *The Rise and Decline of Nations: Economic Growth, Stagflation and Social Rigidities*, New Haven: Yale University Press, 1982.

11 Jan Tinbergen, 'Optimal Development Policies: Lessons from Experience,' *The World Economy*, vol. 7, no. 1 (1984), pp. 112–17.

12 Walter Bagehot, *Economic Studies*, 1876, p. 227.

13   Charles P. Kindleberger, *Economic Growth in France and Britain, 1851–1950*, Cambridge, MA: Harvard University Press, 1964.

Bibliography

Charles P. Kindleberger, 'U.S. Economic Foreign Policy, 1776–1976,' *Foreign Affairs*, vol. 55, no. 2 (1977), pp. 395–417.

10

Afterword

WILLIAM N. PARKER

At the close of a discussion where many voices have voiced many opinions, the audience shuffles out (audiences always seem to shuffle) full of its own thoughts, or perhaps just in a hurry to get to lunch before a line forms. The speakers, a bit dazed, shake hands, receive the chairman's thanks and say a few noncommittal words to one another. When, as in the case of the discussion recorded here, the speakers have directed their remarks toward some positive *end* – in this case to encourage the exposure of economists to economic history – two questions hover in the air: What did they say? and What do we do next?

Of course such questions must be answered by the questioner alone. But it may be useful to consider, before we break up, just what is meant by 'economic history' as the term has been used here. And what can be said to be the value of such a subject in the education of an economist? In the oral discussion at Dallas, and here in the written record, notable agreement appears, I believe on these matters. All the speakers agree that history teaches by example, by 'telling a story' rather than by logical proofs. History's stories are set out in chronological sequences of recorded statements, statistics and purported facts and happenings relating to a circumscribed topic and occurring over a long or short space of time. In history's stories causation is implied but not explicitly stated. The reader or listener is furnished with a 'history' and an 'interpretation' of the course of the events. Such reader or listener must then judge the plausibility of the interpretation set against the reported record and aginst his or her own knowledge of how things move in the world.

The three examples of historical narrative in this book all, I think, exhibit these characteristics. David's history of the typewriter keyboard tells how that set of symbols came to assume and maintain its present form. Temin describes the two types of cross-subsidization in telephone rates and follows out the reasonings within the course of events by which opposite views came to be held. My own introductory discussion describes in a rough time sequence the path travelled by American economics in arriving at the point at which it stands today. The other authors – two theorists and four historian-discussants – would all agree, I think, that these examples are indeed histories. From them, one learns something one could not learn in any other way. Temin and David are emphatic on the importance of the timing and sequence of events in determining an outcome. Arrow and Wright feel that economic history incorporates not only economics, but also other basic social sciences in its narratives and explanations of specific sequences of economic events. Solow agrees, and finds that history suggests hypotheses of behavior which would not normally occur to one whose mental experience had been limited to only one small portion of the historical record. Broadening the base of knowledge and sympathy helps an economist to understand phenomena that seeem to go counter to the norms and assumptions on which standard theory is based, and so allows those theories to be adjusted to accommodate a wider range of economic reality. Rostow appreciates the wider view that a study of history gives the movement of the world economy, showing the elements of regularity and contrast that appear during the course of the historical record. These are necessary ingredients in any effort to understand contemporary life. McCloskey takes the strongest position. He contends that all explanation in the social sciences *is* history: the telling of a plausible story. Theory and statistics are among the means, and sometimes among the most powerful means, to that end. All the authors, of course, say much more than this and agree or disagree at many other points. It is no job of an editor to tell readers what his authors mean. These points, however, are apparent, I think, to any reader and listener and in them the ideas and opinions in the book come together and support one another.

A reader familiar with the 'new' economic history written since 1960 may observe that the view of history as story-telling is not exactly what the 'new' economic historians thought they were doing. A number of the authors here have been explicitly involved in this self-styled 'new' approach. They have used theory and statistics to test historical hypotheses, and nothing said here should be taken to repudiate those methods or deny the value of that enterprise. Statistics form an important body of historical data and require the application of sophisticated techniques to yield up their meaning for a history. The effort to explain the course of economic history – particularly for nineteenth-century America – must rely heavily on many elements of standard economic theory, and the understanding of the subject has, we believe, been much increased by these efforts. But the use of history as a 'testing ground for theory' is only one of its uses and important and valid historical work does not end with explicit applications of econometrics to statistical time series or cross-sectional data from the past.

History indeed is supported by economists on many grounds and utilized by them for many purposes. These emerge most clearly in a departmental meeting where the fate of the economic history requirement in the graduate program is under discussion. For thirty years I have engaged periodically as an extremely interested participant in such discussions. I have observed at least five points around which economists' views seem to cluster. First, history is often said to be a body of data on which theories can be tested, as just mentioned above. There is more data back there than you would imagine, and economists ought not deny themselves access to it. Second, many applied economists in various fields find in the history of that field an abundance of important background information – particularly about the legislative history. In industrial organization one should be aware of the Sherman Act; in agricultural economics, the Agricultural Adjustment Act and its successors. For students of money and banking, some knowledge of the history of the monetary standard and the laws governing banking regulation is not thought amiss. Some modern labor economists even admit to a secret knowledge of the Wagner Act and Taft–Hartley of which they would secretly hope that the new generation would not grow up in ignorance. All this institutional background could be taught piecemeal as part of each applied course. But with the increased use of theory and models in applied courses, it is convenient to have it all taught in one place.

Very different from these reasonings is the support often given to economic history by the theorist, especially by the mathematical theorist. In history, he senses an activity a bit akin in spirit to his own: a delightful occupation of the mind, pursued for its own sake and untainted by immediate considerations of application. Often he is willing to grant history an independence as a form of knowledge, like poetry, intuitive, as original theorizing is intuitive, and possessing no doubt its own rules and rhetoric of verification. Mathematics and history, it is sometimes said, are all that an economics student needs in order to be trained to tackle practical problems. The historian is reluctant to demur from such a flattering opinion, despite the slight uneasiness he feels as he considers the serious methodological and epistemological nightmares that disturb the effort to write valid history.

A fourth line of thought comes from economists actively interested in economic policy on a broad front – from macroeconomists and especially from the development economists. 'He who does not read history is condemned to repeat it,' is the controlling sentiment here, and the view comes in what might be called both a reduced and an extended form. The reduced form is that history is a mine of buried, glittering examples of mankind's earlier mistakes: soil depletion, rampant inflation, environmental pollution, excessive taxes, social misery. As political history is the record of crimes, so economic history is the record of catastrophe abetted by stupidity or greed. The extended form of this sentiment is more sophisticated. Economic development, it says, has occurred over history and is occurring today. Examination of the earlier history of the industrialized portions of the world helps us to see how the process occurred. One learns much about the present by trying to see not simply how it resembles the past in a repetitive pattern, but how also it differs. And finally, opinions of this sort shade ultimately and insensibly into a slightly separate line of thought and impression. History – it is felt – is like foreign travel. It gives its students a broader view of life and a certain wisdom and sophistication that both protects and sensitizes them for the economic world in which they are to spend their professional lives.

The reason for supporting history in the education of an economist then is simply the union of all these sets. So far as I can see, there is little conflict among them. Only the first – that history is a testing ground for theory – fails to give a strong argument for history as a universal requirement alongside theory in a graduate economics program. All applied fields are in one sense testing grounds for theory, and so long as theory confines itself to very short time periods very near the present as it moves forward through time, it has no need, as Solow says, for tests that apply to the bad data of the past the dubious techniques of the present. But of course, if the economist begins to look back or ahead very far, he begins, willy-nilly, to write history. The one attitude, common among many present-minded economists, with which economic history cannot co-exist is the notion that the union of current theory with econometrics provides the only valid approach to knowledge. The historian's story-telling, the authors of this book believe, gives that breadth to the vision and keenness to the intuition which originality in theory making and ingenuity in problem solving inevitably require. And as it does so it also adds – sometimes almost without his realizing it – to the economist's knowledge.

What then of the second of the two questions posed at the outset: what are we to do? The answer, of course, is very simple: expose economists in their student years to classroom work, lectures, even readings, discussions, some research in economic history. Of course not all different qualities desired in the historian can be found in the single scholar who may direct such studies. A department cannot expect to come upon a combination of Schumpeter, Heckscher and Hicks under the skin of one new Ph.D. (older economic historians claim that, like good wine, their flavour improves with age, though, as with hung meat, there is a point beyond which . . .). So long as the economic historian is not indeed a dogmatist of one or another variety, students can read and pick up a variety of information and approaches to history from the course he or she gives. Standard economic history courses also, it should be noted, themselves vary in format and particularly in scope. As Temin's and David's papers show, economic historians are quite interested in explaining specific events. Some consist of a set of such problems, spread out over time, and proceed from the specific historical puzzles – for example, was slavery profitable? – into wider reaches of social and economic circumstances. More traditional courses cover several centuries and are organized in some combination of topics and chronology. Both types of course expose students to the materials and methods of history. Both show how economic life is connected at all its nerve ends to the other systems of social action. Both impress on an economist the significance of the sequences and timing of events in the dynamic changes of economic life.

The speakers in the discussion at Dallas, and all the authors here agree that economists need a generous exposure to economic history as part of their graduate training. This agreement is not surprising. The cards were stacked in favor of such an opinion by the original selection of speakers which Professor Kindleberger and I made. The 'hard-nosed' economist, however, may well pause to ask how a group of presumably sane individuals, with many others, including some of the greatest economic theorists of the past and present, hold these opinions. Hard noses rarely soften until after the age of forty, the limit of eligibility for the J. B. Clark medal. But until then perhaps such economists may be persuaded to feel that they live in a family formed sometime in the distant past by the marriage of theory to a creature of quite a different anatomy, different sensitivities, different modes of problem solving. History needs theory and econometrics to employ all its data and to help it keep its thinking straight. And historical experience can suggest new lines of activity for the minds of theorists. Without theory, history becomes undisciplined and disorganized, shaping its material by whim, or purely by rhetoric. Without history, theory loses any grounding in the actual course of human events. What we are saying here then is, I think, that training economists is a work best accomplished in a family with both parents. Life and education is improved by the contrasts, even the tensions, between them. And everyone is damaged and diminished by a divorce.

Index

Index by Ann Barham